Self-Steering for Yachts

GERARD DIJKSTRA

Self-Steering
for Yachts

Nautical

First published © 1979
by
United Nautical Publishers SA, Basle

This edition published © 1979
by
NAUTICAL PUBLISHING COMPANY LTD
Nautical House, Lymington, Hampshire, England

in association with
George G Harrap & Co Ltd
London

ISBN 0 245 53396 6

Colour separations, printing and binding by
Industrie Grafiche Editoriali Fratelli Pagano, Campomorone, Italy.
Text setting by BAS Printers Limited, Over Wallop, England.

Contents

Illustrations

The photographers were as follows:
William Payne: Cover photo
Franz Weehuizen: 1.3, 1.5, 2.13, 3.6, 4.9, 5.13, 7.6
Theo Kampa: 4.3, 6.9.
Aedgard Koekenbakker: 1.8, 5.10, 7.5
Eileen Ramsay: 1.2
Gerard Dijkstra jr: 1.9, 4.6, 5.6, 5.11, 5.15, 6.1, 6.2, 6.3.
Beken of Cowes: 2.12, 3.4.
Frans van Dusschoten: 3.5.

The Drawings are by Gerard Dijkstra except:
1.11, 5.9: M. S. Gibb Ltd.
5.18: Schwing-Pilot

Foreword

Self-steering gears are complicated and will continue to be so. It is not easy to explain how they work because many factors play a part, particularly in the more sophisticated systems.

The various components which make up a self-steering gear, and the way they interact, are discussed in this book by considering, on the one hand, the individual components themselves and, on the other hand, the complete installation. Self-steering gears are classified at the back of this book with these factors in mind.

A boat is able to steer herself with the help of sails, wind vanes or automatic pilots, but self-steering methods cannot be considered in isolation. They are part of a whole which includes the boat to which they are fitted, and what suits one boat may well not be right for another. All this is discussed, with the emphasis on the relationship between self-steering and the boat (her inherent directional stability). The provision of the power required for automatic pilots is also covered.

The theory behind the various systems and the combination of systems is explained simply, and their effectiveness is evaluated.

It is hoped that reading this book will give an insight into how self-steering systems work, and will help you to decide which is the most suitable system for your boat and the waters where you sail.

1 Wind vane gears

History

Many roads lead to Rome, and this saying is also true of wind vane steering gears. So many different ideas have been tried out and tested that it would need a really thick book to cover all the existing systems. Just a few are covered in this little book, and some of the specific characteristics of these gears are explained more fully. But what is a wind vane steering gear? A few years ago you might possibly have been unable to answer this question, but with the rapid growth in popularity of these 'automatic pilots' there can now be very few sailors unaware of their existence. It seems likely that, within a few years, self-steering gears will have become common and be fitted even to the smallest cruisers. First, however, here is a definition which I would be glad to exchange for a better: 'Wind vane steering gear is an automatic steering system which keeps a boat at a constant angle to the apparent wind when she is under way'.

As with all new equipment for sea-going yachts it is safety and seaworthiness that are the prime considerations, and this is how it should be. Some people consider that wind vane gears meet these requirements—others do not. Originally construction was one of the main objections; the gear generally looked too fragile to withstand a severe storm. This was proved true in certain instances but, now that this method of steering has survived such a hard school, the objection is no longer valid. This hard school is racing single-handed across the Atlantic. The Observer Single-handed Trans-Atlantic Races (OSTAR) have made a major contribution to the development of wind vane gears. No harder test can be imagined and, particularly in the last race in 1976, self-steering gear proved to be increasingly reliable.

It is a very different matter when it comes to using such devices for coastal work or in busy channels. Discretion is essential because irresponsible use of wind vane gears can lead to danger. To go below and leave the boat to steer herself for hours on end is an unhealthy practice in such areas. A sudden change in the wind direction could cause the boat to alter course and head straight for the shore. On the other hand the wind vane can also increase safety in such conditions because the lone sailor is free to navigate or to make a cup of coffee, and he can keep a better lookout. This is equally true when the boat has a small crew; sailing is easier and the crew gets tired less quickly when 'Charly' is at the helm. The wind vane then acts as an untiring member of the crew. And what about its appearance: 'I don't want such a hideous thing on my boat' is a frequent comment when wind vanes are being discussed but, when on watch alone at night with the boat throwing up buckets of spray so that the helm is a very unattractive place to be, many a sailor will be glad of such an ugly object aft, even if only to be able to find a more protected place from which to keep a lookout, or to be able to duck below for a snack.

7

1.1. A Hasler vane gear. The advantages of wind vane gears are obvious from this photograph. The boat is sailing quietly on course while the crea are free to move about on deck. Self-steering gear is not only useful for ocean voyages but also when cruising at sea at weekends with a small crew.

Wind vanes were first used in about 1920 to steer model yachts during races, the power developed by the vane always being transmitted direct to the rudder. Strangely enough the first full-scale wind vane was fitted to a motor yacht nearly 14 metres in length. Marin Marie used it aboard *Arielle* when crossing the Atlantic in 1939. It was not until 1955 that effective wind vanes made their appearance aboard sailing boats. Ian Major's *Buttercup* and Michael Henderson's *Mick the Miller* being the pioneers. However it was really the Single-handed Trans-Atlantic Races that inspired development. H. G. Hasler with *Jester*, a junk-rigged Folkboat, was deeply involved in the development of wind vanes, and it was he who introduced pendulum vane gears. Nor was interest confined to Britain. The French engineer Marcel Gianoli was the first to produce a wind vane that rotated about a horizontal rather than a vertical axis. Since then many successful ocean passages have been made during which wind vanes have proved their worth, such as the circumnavigations via Cape Horn by Bill Nance, Sir Francis Chichester and Sir Alec Rose.

When can vane gears be used?

Ideally wind vane steering gears should be able to steer as well as, or better than, the best helmsman on board in all conditions that arise. That may well sound an impossibly high aim, but it appears that vane gears can satisfy this requirement on various points of sailing. Furthermore the wind vane does not get tired, and that is a claim that not even the best of helmsmen can make.

A vane gear works best on a close hauled course, simply because most boats tend to sail themselves in any case when on the wind. When this characteristic is combined with self-steering gear a boat can sail a better course to windward than a human helmsman. The wind vane reacts to every slight change in the wind, including the slants which a helmsman might perhaps not notice in a heavy swell. This is particularly true at night or when the helmsman starts to get tired.

Obviously a self-steering gear cannot predict the boat's reactions to gusts and waves, and can only correct the boat when she goes off course, whereas a helmsman can anticipate. He can often apply the helm before the boat goes off course, especially when on a broad reach or a run, and will then steer a better course than a wind vane because he can see the approaching waves and anticipate the boat's reactions. Even then a wind vane will perform better than a poor or tired helmsman.

Problems can arise when the boat is running very fast in high seas. Vanes may lose the wind temporarily due to the lack of wind in wave troughs, and also when the boat starts to surge forward on the crests, as often happens with multihulls. These boats can sail so fast that boat

1.2 *One of the pioneers of single-handed sailing is seen here well equipped for sailing alone. This is* JESTER *at the start of the 1960 Observer Single-handed Trans-Atlantic Race, with a trim tab vane gear fitted. Col. H. G. Hasler later used her to try out his pendulum vane gear.* JESTER *is the only boat to have competed in all the OSTARS—no mean performance for a Folkboat.*

1.3. BRITISH STEEL *is one of the largest boats ever fitted with a Hasler vane gear. Chay Blyth sailed her round the world non-stop against the prevailing winds. Half way round a wave sweeping over the boat buckled the tubular frame to which the steering gear was attached and Chay Blyth had to complete the voyage without the vane's help. This photo shows* BRITISH STEEL *at the start of the 1972 OSTAR in which Brian Cooke finished fourth. The Hasler gear was the forerunner of pendulum vane gears, and more advanced types are now on the market.*

speed exceeds wind speed and the vane consequently cannot steer the boat. The direction of the apparent wind is also changed by this sudden increase in boat speed and, because the wind vane steers the boat in relation to the apparent wind, the boat will turn to a course different from that desired. Multihulls suffer greatly from this, both in surfing conditions and when sailing with the sheets slightly eased. Bearing away a little can then cause a marked increase in boat speed and steering is badly affected. A reach in light airs is another difficult course for a wind vane when a sea is running. When the boat yaws the apparent wind is affected so much that it no longer indicates the direction of the course correctly. These problems and possible solutions are considered in greater detail in chapter 2.

The main requirement is to be able to steer the boat in extreme conditions, not only with a view to making fast ocean passages but also to avoid gybing or broaching. A boat steered by a wind vane does not follow a dead straight course but sails slightly to either side of it, the average course coinciding with the course selected. For example a boat will keep within five degrees either side of her proper course when close hauled, but within ten degrees when running. These figures vary, of course, but give some indication of the performance that can be expected from a wind vane in normal circumstances. Naturally much will depend on the behaviour and directional stability of the boat herself in a seaway.

Self-steering gear is no longer in its infancy. Development is in full swing and it appears that a new era is dawning for cruising boats. Long spells at the helm are dwindling and being replaced by more enjoyable sailing. What self-steering gears

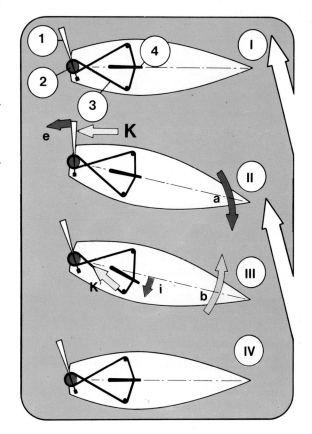

1.4. *This is how a wind vane gear works.*
I *The boat is on course with the wind slightly forward of the beam.*
II *The boat goes off course and her longitudinal axis moves in direction* **a**. *This causes the vane to stand at a slight angle to the wind which now exerts force K on the vane, trying to push it in a direction* **e** *to line up with the wind direction.*
III *This results in force K¹ being exerted on the tiller line which deflects the tiller in a direction* **i**, *making the boat bear away to port and back to her original course, her longitudinal axis moving in direction* **b**.
IV *Everything is back as before and the boat is on course again. Although the diagrams show this broken down into stages everything occurs simultaneously in one smooth movement in practice.*

It will also now be understood how the wind vane can put a boat about. When the vane is turned through 90° and recoupled to the steering system the boat will follow the vane, go about, and take up her new course at right angles to the old course, leaving the helmsman's hands free to man the sheets and so on. A fuller description of a wind vane that works in this way and is easy to make at home will be found in the chapter on 'Home construction of wind vane gears'.
Key: *1, wind vane. 2, rotating turret on which the vane is mounted, and drum for the tiller lines. 3, tiller lines. 4, tiller.*

The vane is coupled to the drum. When not being used to steer it is uncoupled and is then free to rotate with the wind. To operate the gear bring the boat on to the course desired, let the vane turn to align with the wind and then couple the vane to the drum. The vane will steer the boat as described above.

cannot do is to think ahead. They cannot see sudden squalls approaching or storm clouds gathering, nor will they spot the lights of a steamer on a collision course, or waves breaking over a shoal ahead. A self-steering gear can do many things, but one thing it is not—it is not an automatic lookout.

Reliability

Wind vanes can be assumed to be reliable under normal circumstances. The well-known makes have been thoroughly tested and quality is such that they can deal satisfactorily with the forces involved when steering a boat. Vulnerable parts such as the pendulum or the vane must be easy to replace. Most pendulums have a fail-safe device in case they run into flotsam, the pendulum being released by a spring catch instead of breaking. Auxiliary rudders are attached with shear bolts so that, should such overloading occur that the auxiliary rudder could break, the bolts will shear before the rudder itself is damaged (remember to take spare bolts with you).

The tiller lines can also be weak links. They will chafe badly if they are too thin, if the sheaves are too narrow or if the lead is poor, particularly When considerable force is required to move the boat's helm. The lead of the lines requires much thought when vane gear is fitted. Using large sheaves and flexible rope made up of long fibres, and applying talc or grease when chafe threatens, helps to solve the problem.

A wind vane can be damaged during a heavy storm however, not when it is steering the boat but, generally, when it is not operating, for example when the boat is hove to. Waves breaking aboard can unship or break the vane gear. Water pressure when the boat is being driven astern in a storm can unship the auxiliary rudder and the pendulum.

Breakable components such as vane and pendulum ought to break (or the fail-safe device should give) before the framework is damaged. Auxiliary rudders etc should be disengaged when not in use so that they can turn freely in the water. Yielding to pressure is preferable to breaking.

Heavy, solid-looking gears present a larger surface area to breaking seas and, in the long run, may be less reliable than lighter gears which are less vulnerable to waves, water pressure and the forces of inertia that result when the boat's stern swings wildly. It must be possible to replace components, while the frame, which is irreplaceable unless a complete spare gear is carried on board, must be very strong.

How they work

All types of wind vane gears on the market have one thing in common—the wind vane actuates the rudder and thus steers the boat. The vane stands at a constant angle to the wind, and when the boat deviates from her course the wind holds the vane steady. Therefore when the boat alters course the wind vane turns in relation to the centreline of the boat. (It is actually the boat that turns while the wind vane remains steady.) This change of angle is now transmitted to the rudder or auxiliary rudder, and the vane moves the rudder in such a way as to bring the boat back to her old course. In other words, the angle between the apparent wind and the boat's centreline reverts to its original value.

Although the wind vane can move the rudder directly, the force required is often far too great. Several methods have been devised of increasing the power developed by the wind vane by means of the linkage used between vane and rudder, and it is largely in the way that the linkage is effected that the individual types of vane gears differ noticeably from each other.

1.5. *Very simple vane gears can be used for smaller boats. This is the* QME *vane fitted to* JUSTA LISTANG *seen at the start of the 1972 OSTAR.*

The tiller is operated by a horizontally pivoted vane. A pendulum vane gear would perform better than this installation but is considerably more expensive.

1.6. *A convincing photo of the Windpilot at work. This is the simplest model of Windpilot, the vane being connected directly to the helm by the tiller line. Note the lever on top of the tiller where the tiller line is made fast to the helm. The course is set with the wing nut on top of the vane's vertical pivot.*

Systems

A: Vane gears which act directly on the rudder (1.5)

Although this is far and away the cheapest and simplest method performance can be satisfactory but, because the wind vane generates little power, this system is only suitable for small boats that are light on the helm. Larger and very cumbersome wind vanes are needed when a good deal of power is required to steer the boat, and the self-steering gear used by Chichester in the 1960 OSTAR was an example. The wind vane staff fitted to *Gipsy Moth III* was so large that it looked more

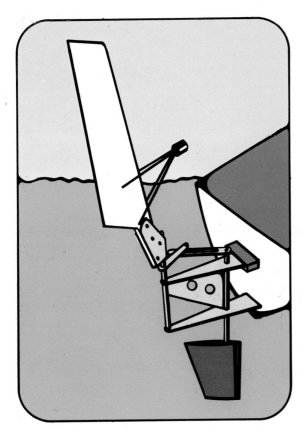

1.7. *The Automate vane gear. This is the simplest wind vane gear to use an auxiliary rudder, and is suitable for boats up to 3 tons displacement. It is hung on the stern like an outboard.*

1.8. GAULOISES *at the start of the 1976 OSTAR. This 17·5 metre boat is also being steered without difficulty by a wind vane. A small vane with a slightly inclined horizontal axis actuates a pendulum through differential linkage, and the pendulum in turn actuates the tiller. The efficiency of this Atoms vane gear is very certainly mainly due to the accurate and nearly friction-free construction of the linkage between vane and pendulum.*

1.9. PEN DUICK IV's *self-steering gear designed by Marcel Gianoli. Crew members make a minor repair to the trim tab before the start of the 1968 OSTAR. The wind vane pivots about a slightly inclined horizontal axis and actuates the trim tab on the main rudder through a differential linkage.*

This is a complicated and expensive gear based on the MNOP, but the vane actuates the main rudder instead of an auxiliary rudder. The MNOP steering gear differs from other gears in that the vane is linked, via a trim tab, to a main or auxiliary rudder which is overbalanced.

like a mizzen mast, and the vane was actually a small sail that could even be reefed. For the next race four years later this impractical device had been replaced by Hasler vane gear. Nevertheless, as has been said, this is a thoroughly practicable system for small boats and is extremely suitable for home construction.

B: Vane gears that actuate a small auxiliary rudder (see fig. 1.7)

The demands made on the rudder by the vane are a great deal lower than those made when manoeuvring, let alone when reaching under spinnaker.

A small auxiliary rudder, perhaps a quarter of the size of the main rudder, is quite large enough to keep the boat on course and requires considerably less steering force, particularly if a balanced rudder is used as is generally the case. The auxiliary rudder is fitted right aft, and this increases its effect. The turning moment is greater without more steering force being required, while the friction and inertia of such steering gears are lower. Tabarly used this system in *Pen Duick II, III* and *IV*. An auxiliary rudder can be recommended for boats whose directional stability is poor, the main rudder is then fixed in the position which

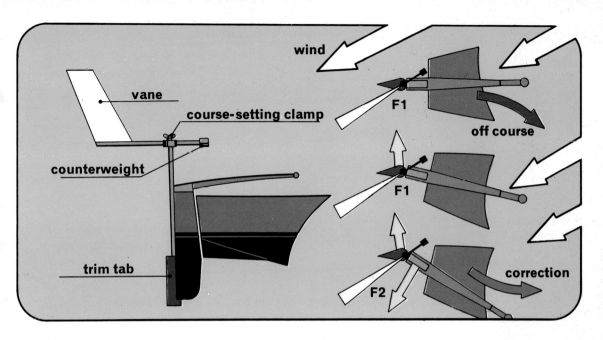

1.10. *This is the simplest possible self-steering system using a wind vane and trim tab. A counterweight is fitted to the vane to ensure that it stays balanced, even when the boat is heeling because, due to gravity, the vane would otherwise exert force on the steering system whenever the boat heeled, and this would lead to an undesired change of course. The principle is simple: the trim tab is balanced so that even the slightest force exerted by the wind vane will correct the boat's course. When the boat goes off course the angle of the wind vane to the boat's centreline alters, and causes the trim tab, which is clamped to the vane by a wing nut, to turn across the waterflow. The waterflow exerts force F1 on the rudder through the trim tab, causing the rudder to turn and force F2 to arise. This is so directed that the boat is turned back to her old course. F2 is always greater than F1 so that the force F2 minus F1 causes the boat to turn to port. It is important that the correction is made with only a moderate deflection of the rudder*

and, in practice, the swing of the tiller has to be limited. The arc through which the tiller swings can be restricted by attaching elastic bands either side of the tiller.

More sophisticated systems use differential linkage which incorporates the two following characteristics. First the linkage ratio between vane and trim tab is not 1:1 as in this simple design. Trim tab deflection is reduced to a fraction of the wind vane's deflection. Second, when the rudder deflects further the trim tab is brought back almost in line with the rudder or, at least, the angle between trim tab and rudder does not increase as it does here because the latter leads to wild and irregular steering.

The method of balancing the trim tab shown here cannot be recommended. The part that projects forward below the rudder is vulnerable and could easily be fouled by rope or weed. A more satisfactory method of balancing is used, for example, for Crew vane gears. (see pp. 80/81).

keeps the boat as well balanced as possible so that the auxiliary rudder has the minimum of work to do. A second rudder of this type also considerably increases the stability of the whole steering system.

C: Vane gears which actuate a trim tab that moves the rudder (see fig. 1.10)

The wind vane actuates the trim tab, the trim tab actuates the rudder and the rudder steers the boat.

Here the force of the waterflow is used to move the rudder and, in spite of a smaller wind vane, much greater steering power is available than with the systems just described. Installation is extremely simple when boats have a rudder hung at the stern and, until very recently, it was such boats in particular that fitted self-steering gears. This is a very simple and inexpensive solution for boats with stern-hung rudders, and is very suitable for home construction.

This system is not only popular for boats with rudders hung at the stern. *Pen Duick IV* and *Raph*, both boats with 'normal' rudders, used wind vanes which operated trim tabs on their main rudders, but the linkage between vane and rudder then becomes very complicated and expensive. Regall steering gear, as used aboard *Pen Duick V*, is a further development. The vane actuates a trim tab on an auxiliary rudder, so making construction easier with vane and auxiliary rudder combined as a single unit.

D: Pendulum wind vane gears (see fig. 1.11)

Although this is the last type to be mentioned it is certainly not the least important. Hasler was the pioneer in this field. In the 1972 OSTAR five of the first seven competitors to finish used pendulum vane gears, and in 1976 they were fitted to the majority of the fleet. The vane again actuates a trim tab but this trim tab, the pendulum, is now an independent component that sticks down into the water like a paddle and turns about both a vertical

and a horizontal axis. When the vane turns, the pendulum is turned simultaneously at an angle to the waterflow which exerts a lateral force on the pendulum and, because it can swing about its horizontal axis (in line with the boat's centreline), the pendulum is forced sideways. This movement is then transmitted to the rudder.

1.11. *The sketch shows the principle of the pendulum wind vane gear developed by Blondie Hasler and marketed by Gibb. The change in the vane's angle (1) is transmitted to the servo-blade (5) through the course setting latch gear (2) and linkage (3). The servo-blade or pendulum turns about its vertical axis across the waterflow. The resultant side force (f) on the pendulum causes it to swing sideways about its horizontal axis (4) and this movement is transmitted through the tiller line (6) to the rudder. Although the system appears complicated it is exceptionally satisfactory in practice and is one of the best tried systems available at present.*

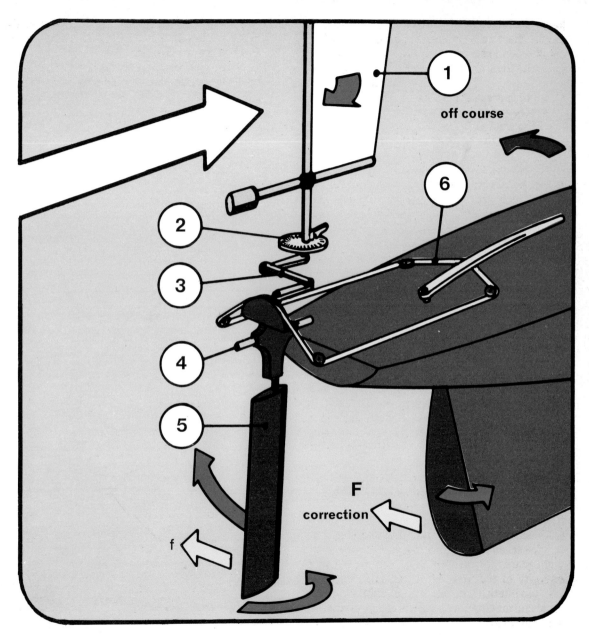

off course

F
correction

f

2 Components of wind vane gears

The vane

The first vanes to appear at sea pivoted about a vertical axis like a weathercock. Although this type of wind vane steering gear can work very well it has its disadvantages. Whenever this conventional vane reacts to the boat's change of course it 'loses' the wind while the course is being corrected, the wind pressure on it decreasing as the vane turns away from the wind. A vane that turns about a horizontal axis does not have this trouble; it is pushed over like the sail of a windmill and does not lose the wind as it moves. A deviation from course therefore causes much greater vane movement, and consequently a vane with a horizontal axis generates more power to move the rudder than a conventional vane.

The axis of a horizontally pivoted vane has to be inclined at a slight angle if the vane is to deflect to a degree that is in proportion to the degree that the boat deviates from her course. (This happens automatically with a conventional vane.) Figure 2.1 illustrates this. The apparent wind in figure A alters as indicated by c, causing the vane to swing through a similar angle b. It is assumed that boat speed here does not change as a result of the boat going off her original course. Figure B illustrates the relationship between angle c and angle b.

$$\text{Tan } b = \frac{c}{\sin a}$$

If $a = 6\cdot5°$, $b = 8\cdot5\,c$. In other words, given the same alteration c in the apparent wind direction, the vane will move through a much greater angle than the vane in figure A. Because the vane flaps right over every time the course is altered, and angle b is therefore no longer determined by angle c, a vane with $a = 0$ can be used for a self-steering gear, but with such a horizontally pivoted vane it is then often necessary to limit rudder deflection to avoid oversteering.

A vane with an approximately horizontal axis can be smaller due to the greater power generated and, consequently, both vane and counter-weight can be lighter. This reduces inertia and increases sensitivity.

How the wind acts on the vane

The force exerted on a wind vane and the force produced, R in figure 2.2, depend on the angle of the vane to the wind. This is called the angle of incidence. The graph shows how the force produced varies according to the angle of incidence. When the vane is in line with the wind no force is produced, and when the boat goes only slightly off course, say 5°, R barely increases. However, if the vane is set at a slight angle of incidence when the boat is on course any deviation from that course will have a much greater effect, the vane will steer more positively and react more quickly. Positive weather helm is therefore desir-

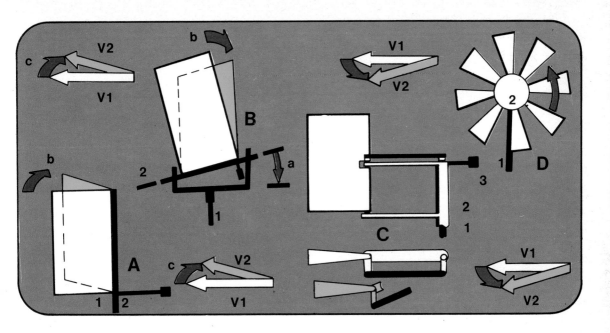

able because, to keep the boat on course, the vane will have to exert a certain force to counter the tendency to luff up. The vane is therefore set at a slight angle to the wind and will react instantly to every slight shift. If the boat is too well balanced it is probably advisable to introduce some weather helm deliberately and give the rudder some bias by attaching elastic to the tiller, for example, so that the vane has to counter this pressure on the helm.

The vane's profile shape greatly affects its sensitivity and reactions to deviations from course. Most vanes are just flat pieces of wood and seem to work satisfactorily, but a closer investigation into the most suitable profile shapes for vanes seems to be needed. There is little sense in shaping wooden boards because the result will be that the vane has too thin a cross section.

Several alternatives are shown in figure 2.3 and it appears that the vanes with flaps perform best. At small angles of incidence all these shapes

2.1   *Types of wind vane:*

A: Vertically pivoted vane. Altering course through angle c *causes the vane to turn through a similar angle* b.

B: Vane with slightly inclined horizontal axis (angle a*). Altering course through angle* c *causes the vane to swing through angle* b *the ratio being* $Tan\ \mathbf{b} = \mathbf{c}/sin\ \mathbf{a}$.

C: Vane with dual vertical axes. This is more powerful than a normal vertically pivoted vane because it does not lose the wind as it moves.

D: Windmill vane. This can generate a great deal of power. The vane is set parallel to the wind direction and any deviation from course turns it via gearing either to the right or to the left. This type of vane may have a heavy outer ring, and will then be set across the wind direction, the course being corrected by gyroscopic action.

Key: *1, course setting axis. 2, vane axis. 3, counterweight. V1, wind direction. V2, wind direction as a result of the boat going off course.*

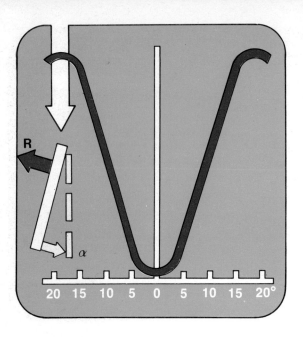

2.2. *This graph shows the relationship between the angle of the vane to the wind (the angle of incidence) and the associated force, R, produced by the vane as a result of that wind.*
It can be seen that the maximum force is exerted when the vane is at an angle of about 18°.

are an improvement on flat wooden vanes.

Various manufacturers prefer wedge-shaped wind vanes, those with two flaps being the most powerful and the most sensitive. There must be a gap between the flap and the vane, just as with the flaps used when an aeroplane lands.

A vane will exert greatest force at an angle of incidence of about 18°. When the angle increases the vane stalls and loses power. This is due to the breakaway of the airflow on the lee side of the vane, just as is experienced by aircraft wings. When there is a major alteration in course the conventional wind vane stalls and can exert little force to bring the boat back on course. A vane that pivots about a slightly inclined horizontal axis has less trouble because the angle of incidence will be no greater than the angle of its axis to the horizontal when it is forced over to its fullest extent and is therefore practically horizontal.

There are no limits to the size of the vane. If a vane is sufficiently powerful at wind force 2 it will serve for all higher wind speeds. Only constructional considerations may make it necessary to ship a smaller vane during a storm.

Air pressure on the vane varies as the square of wind speed, and the consequences of this are shown in figure 2.4, a polar performance diagram such as is often used for yachts. Vs indicates boat speed and direction on various points of sailing related to the true wind's direction, Vt. The vane does not actually experience the true wind but the apparent wind that results from the effect of boat speed on the true wind. The apparent wind is indicated by curve Va. When the boat is close hauled the apparent wind is stronger than the true wind, but it is considerably less strong on downwind courses. Because air pressure is related to the square of wind speed the difference between the true wind and the apparent wind causes a drastic change in R, the force produced, and R is

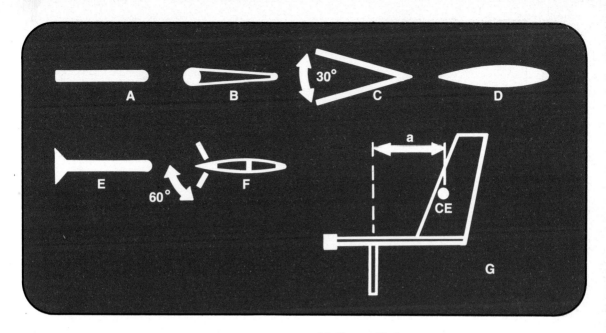

greatest when the boat is close hauled and best able to steer herself. Unfortunately R is greatly reduced when the boat is reaching and running, just when more power is needed to steer her. Sadly this is unavoidable. The vane has to be large enough to deliver adequate steering power when the wind is free, although a smaller vane would suffice when the boat is close hauled.

Figure 2.1 shows an alteration of angle c to the apparent wind causing a similar alteration of angle b at the wind vane, but in practice this is not the case because a change in course can affect the speed of the boat as well as the direction of the apparent wind. In figure 2.5 a boat is sailing close hauled at 7 knots. Vt indicates the direction and speed of the true wind while Va indicates the apparent wind. What happens now when the boat bears away off course? Boat speed increases as the wind frees and, in the case illustrated, because bearing away 15° adds one knot to boat speed the

2.3. Vane profile shapes.

A   *Flat board, the most widely used type of vane.*

B   *Wedge-shaped cross-section, the vane consisting of two tubes over which sail cloth is stretched. The smaller section tube forms the leading edge. This stiff light vane is more sensitive than the flat board to alterations in wind direction.*

C   *The wide wedge is made from two flat plates. This type is very sensitive to small changes in wind direction, but it does not look so neat and furthermore it has a higher wind resistance when not in use than other types.*

D   *A streamlined vane is more powerful and stalls later than a flat board. A symmetrical aerofoil profile shape can be used for vanes when both sides turn into the wind, as is the case with some horizontally pivoted vanes.*

E   *Spoilers. Increased vane sensitivity results from adding a small wedge to the trailing edge of the vane.*

F   *Flaps. The most effective wind vane profile shape combines streamlining with flaps set at an angle of 60° to the centreline of the vane. The length of the flaps is about 20% of the chord (breadth). A small gap must be left between flap and vane.*

G   *Both the area of the vane and the distance **a** between the vane and its axis determine the power it generates. The force produced acts through the centre of pressure at about a quarter of the chord length. The further this centre is from the axis the greater the vane's turning moment.*

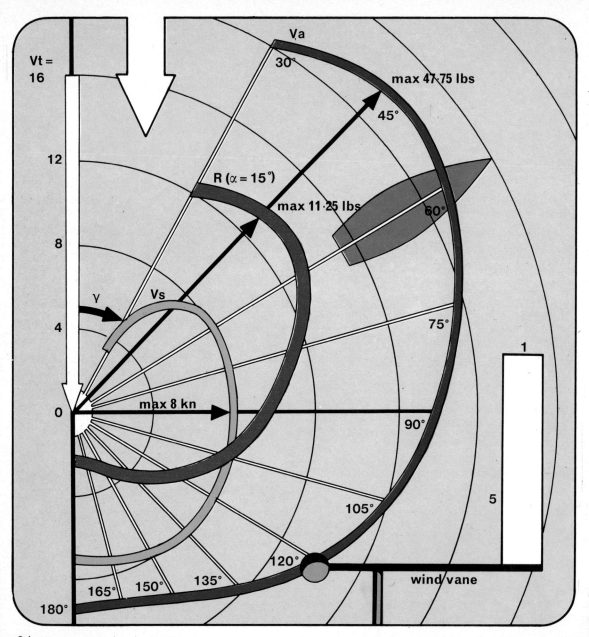

2.4. *This polar diagram shows the degree of force, R, produced by the vane on different points of sailing related to a constant true wind. The wind vane is a flat board, one square metre in area, and the angle of incidence, α, is 15°. Because pressure changes as the square of wind speed the power that a vane can exert when the boat is off the wind is very much lower than that exerted when she is close hauled.*

Key: *Vt, true wind. Va, apparent wind. Vs, boat speed. R, force produced. Y, course. In the example Vt = 16 knots.*

angle of the apparent wind alters only 9°. The correction required from the vane steering gear is therefore less than would be expected from the degree of deviation from course, but no matter, the wind vane is sensitive enough to deal with this.

It is a different matter when the same vane is fitted to a multihull because these boats can accelerate very suddenly. A minor deviation from her course at a critical moment can help the boat to start planing. Such a situation is shown in figure 2.6 where it is evident that the vane completely loses the ability to correct the course, and the result is a multihull 'breakaway'. The boat cannot be steered by the wind vane. When the increase in boat speed is greater than that shown in figure 2.6 the course can even be 'corrected' in the wrong direction.

The situation is different when boat speed increases due to the wind strengthening. The direction of the apparent wind will then change and the boat will bear away wrongly from her course. This can also happen in a high sea when the boat starts to surf on wave crests, and again the vane will not be able to steer the boat.

Using boat speed as sensor

A way is being sought of countering this phenomenon by incorporating changes in boat speed into the self-steering system so that they help to keep the boat on course. To sense direction the

wind vane ought to be set in relation to the true wind, rather than to the apparent wind. This is no problem with an electronic automatic pilot. It is easy enough to feed information on boat speed and apparent wind to a small computer that calculates the direction of the true wind, which is then used as the signal for the automatic pilot. More needs to be done before a similar system is available for wind vane gears and it is at present only possible to resort to palliative measures when conditions are extremely difficult.

The Hasler steering gear provides a partial solution to the problem when surfing. This was discovered by chance by Bill Howell sailing his boat *Golden Cockerel* during the 1968 OSTAR. Whenever the boat started to plane the force of the water acting backwards on the pendulum was so great that the entire pendulum and its attachments tilted slightly, in so far as the mountings permitted. The force of the water streaming past the pendulum far exceeds that exerted by the wind vane, and the vane can no longer turn the pendulum in response to the undesired shift in the apparent wind's direction caused by the boat starting to surf. It seemed possible to keep the boat under control when surfing because the vane had no effect as she surged off the top of a wave and the water rushing past the pendulum stabilised the rudder. When boat speed dropped in the troughs the pendulum reverted to its upright position and the vane resumed control of steering. Hasler now markets an adaptation so that the gear can be

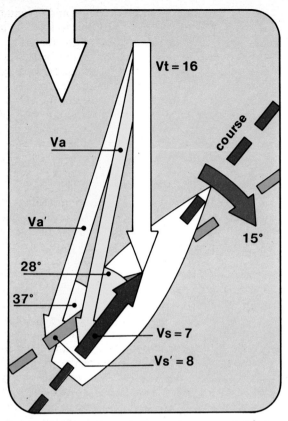

Vt = 16

Va

course

15°

Va'

28°

37°

Vs = 7

Vs' = 8

2.5. *Wind vane reaction to a change of course coupled with a small increase in boat speed. Bearing away 15° increases boat speed by one knot, and the apparent wind shifts 9°. The wind vane therefore has to react to a much smaller change in the angle of the apparent wind than might be expected.*

fitted to the sterns of multihulls with a hinged bracket.

A more adaptable method of using boat speed as a signal is to tow a warp which, for example, can be made fast to the tiller or to the pendulum. The drag on the warp in the water varies with boat speed, and this variation in force is used to influence the steering gear in such a way that the change in boat speed counters the effect of the shift in the apparent wind. A short thin warp is enough to influence the steering gear if it is attached to a pendulum or a trim tab. It can be made fast to a trim tab or pendulum arm in the same way as the vane is attached, or can be led to the vane blade itself. The length of line required to produce the force needed to influence vane movement has to be found by experiment. Some ingenuity is called for if the wind vane gear is to function in extreme conditions, but the method described above increases the range of conditions in which wind vanes can be used.

The effect on the vane of rolling, heeling and yawing

The wind's control of the vane is also affected by rolling and yawing, the former only being important when running downwind with the wind vane installed high, say at the top of the mast. Rolling has no adverse effect on the apparent wind and can be used to damp down yawing and rolling on a run. An electronic automatic pilot can make use of this characteristic provided that an extra sensor, such as a compass or a wind vane fitted lower down, is coupled into the system.

Yawing influences the apparent wind more because the effect is further from the point about which the boat turns. Figure 2.7 shows what happens to the vane when the stern swings. The sideways movement of the stern causes the vane to meet a wind as indicated by vector Vp. This vector

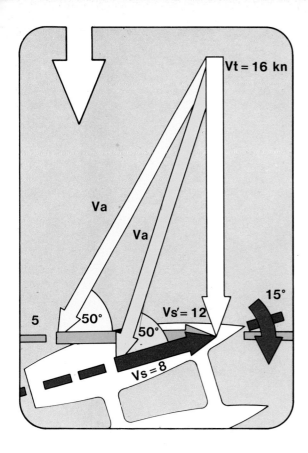

2.6. *This figure shows the same situation as that in the figure opposite except that the wind vane here is fitted to a multihull. These boats can accelerate very quickly as a result of a following sea, of bearing away and so on, and an increase in boat speed from eight to twelve knots is far from hypothetical. The disastrous consequence for the vane gear can be seen in the vector diagram where the direction of the apparent wind does not change at all when the boat bears away 15°, and the wind vane therefore does not correct the course. If boat speed increases even further the vane will cause the rudder to deflect the wrong way and the boat will deviate even further from her course. A multihull 'breakaway' will be the result and the vane cannot control the boat. The only steering systems that can be used in these circumstances are those that, by one means or another, make use of boat speed Vs as a control signal to keep the boat on course.*

has to be added to the apparent wind, and the wind that determines the vane's position is Va^1. On a close hauled course this results in a greater change in the direction of Va relative to the boat and, consequently, in more powerful course correction. Unfortunately Vp has the opposite effect on a run, and less power is available to correct the course just when it is badly needed. When sailing off the wind in a seaway in light airs Vp can be so great by comparison with Va that there can be no question of the wind vane correcting the course. Something other than a vane is then needed to correct yawing unless the vane is fitted on the foredeck.

Few boats counter yawing automatically, but the few steering systems that do produce the desired damping effect either use a pendulum, or an overbalanced rudder or auxiliary rudder, which meets a lateral waterflow when the boat swings. The resultant force is used to move the rudder to counter the swing.

The increase in the boat's angle of heel in a gust also causes difficulties for wind vane gears. Unless extra force is applied to the helm most boats luff up when they heel further and the sails then have to be retrimmed and/or the wind vane setting adjusted. This is a nuisance in gusty weather. One solution is to fit a special counterweight on a lever ahead of the axis of the pendulum, trim tab or wind vane so that, when the boat heels, the weight deflects the rudder, causing it to produce the counter-pressure required to keep the boat on course.

Few vane gears use this method because it seems that the counterweight has to be adjusted to every change of wind. The vane itself has a normal counterweight, however, to prevent gravity affecting its position. This keeps the vane in equilibrium and vane deflection therefore does not change when the boat heels.

The efficiency of an auxiliary rudder or pendulum hung on the stern is reduced when the boat heels because it lifts partly out of the water

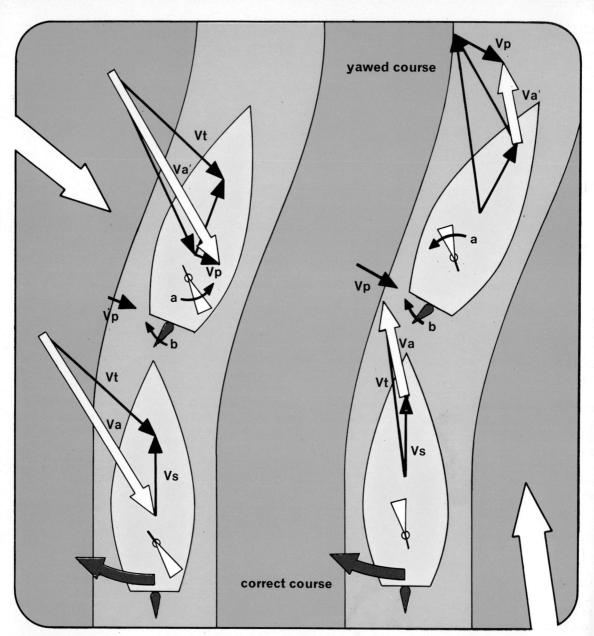

yawed course

correct course

28

2.7. How yawing affects a wind vane installed aft. Vp, the wind caused by the sideways motion of the stern, increases the sensitivity of the steering gear on close hauled course, but reduces sensitivity when the wind is free. When the boat is running in a seaway in light weather Vp can become so strong that the vane cannot indicate the course. Only types of self-steering gear which automatically damp down yawing effects will be able to steer a boat in such conditions.

when the boat heels and does not counter the extra weather helm automatically.

Spaniel, the successful Polish competitor in the 1976 OSTAR, used two angled rudders, the area of which altered in the simplest possible way (figure 2.13). As the boat heeled further the leeward rudder was more deeply immersed but the effective area of the windward rudder was reduced, with the result that the leeward rudder generated more steering force and thus automatically compensated for the increased weather helm. Although her vane gear was superior in this respect the combination of a horizontally pivoted vane and a balanced auxiliary rudder does not produce the best results.

The wind vane steering gears with an inherent ability to counter yawing rely on this to compensate for increased weather helm before the boat has deviated so far from her course that the vane has to make a correction.

Obviously it is always preferable if the hull design is such that the boat does not gripe when she heels.

Trim tab and pendulum

The simplest vane gears are those with wind vanes that actuate the main or auxiliary rudder of a yacht directly, but in most cases the power generated by the movement of the wind vane has to be augmented and, as already stated, a trim tab or a pendulum is used for this purpose. Figure 2.8 gives the proportions of some trim tabs and their rudders. Just as with wind vanes, the further the trim tab is from the rudder pivot the greater the effect of the trim tab on the rudder.

In figure 2.10A deflection a of the wind vane causes deflection b at the trim tab. The linkage ratio is $1:1$, in other words angle a equals angle b. The linkage ratio can be altered by varying the length of the lever. This deflection of the wind vane causes the trim tab to set slightly across the waterflow which exerts force f on the trim tab. The resulting couple $f \times l$ moves the rudder, which, deflecting in turn, experiences force F and a similar but contrary couple results, $F \times L$. As l is longer than L, F is greater than f, and the difference between these forces is the turning moment that steers the boat. The work of the rudder is reduced when a trim tab is fitted because the resultant steering force F minus f is always less than force F which would be available for steering were there no trim tab. The demands self-steering gears make on a rudder are less than those made when manoeuvring, so this reduction in steering power requirement is no disadvantage although it comes at the cost of increased resistance. A state of equilibrium has to be set up between trim tab and rudder so that trim tab deflection relates to rudder deflection. This state of equilibrium should exist when trim tab and rudder are similarly deflected, that is to say, when the angle between the boat's

Continued on page 32

2.8. Rudders—balanced, partially balanced and overbalanced:

Note *The terms used by the author to describe rudders accord with the definitions given by John S. Letcher in his book 'Self-steering for sailing craft'. An unbalanced rudder is a flap rudder hinged along the leading edge. A balanced rudder has part of the area forward of the axis about which it pivots. With a partially balanced rudder the axis is forward of the centre of pressure through which the lift force is generated. With a completely balanced rudder the axis passes through the centre of pressure. With an overbalanced rudder the centre of pressure is forward of the axis.*

A *Overbalanced rudder with trim tab. This is the MNOP auxiliary rudder. When the vane is operating the rudder rotates about axis 1 and axis 2 is locked. When the wind vane is not being used but the rudder is required to counter yawing, axis 1 is locked and the rudder pivots about axis 2, aligning itself with the waterflow, and presenting the minimum of resistance. 3 is the differential linkage between the vane and the trim tab which is also balanced. End-plates top and bottom increase rudder efficiency.*

B PEN DUICK IV's *rudder works on the same principle as the MNOP gear, and both were designed by Marcel Gianoli. This rudder is equally suitable for vane or manual steering.*

C *A partially balanced auxiliary rudder with trim tab. The 12·5% of the rudder area forward of the axis is on the low side, but this can be increased to 20% if desired. This would very definitely be necessary if the auxiliary rudder were directly linked to a wind vane without the intermediary of a trim tab. The differential linkage shown is suitable for a vertically pivoted vane. 4, vane pivot, mounted on the boat. 5, vane arm. 6, bolt. 7, slotted arm. The linkage ratio between vane and rudder can be altered by moving bolt 6 along vane arm 5.*

D *Trim tab fitted to a rudder hung on the transom with a skeg, showing suitable proportions.*

E *A main rudder with a flap similar to that used for aeroplane wings. This type of rudder is suitable for vane steering because, although little power is needed to move the flap, the steering force generated is very great. There is no vulnerable linkage such as that associated with a trim tab.*

F *Trim tab fitted to a flap rudder hinged to a long keel. Linkage to this type of trim tab is vulnerable and cannot be repaired at sea. A hollow rudder stock is often used for parts of the linkage.*

G *A trim tab's efficiency can be improved by adding spoilers along the trailing edge. The trim tab area is correct if the angle between the trim tab and the rudder blade corresponds to the degree of deflection of the rudder.*

H *Like the rudders in A and B the Mustafà wind vane's rudder is overbalanced. When not in use the rudder is not free to turn in the water but is locked in line with the boat's fore-and-aft axis. It can also be used as the main rudder and manual steering is possible.*

I *The Sailomat wind vane's rudder is not served by a trim tab but by a pendulum. This is a completely balanced rudder but it appears that it might even be overbalanced if sufficiently immersed. The pendulum balances the rudder in the same way as the trim tabs at A, B and H, but its effect is greater. Pendulums and trim tabs increase the effect of overbalanced rudders, but the force generated by a trim tab reduces the effect of a conventional rudder. This is considered further in figure 2.10.*

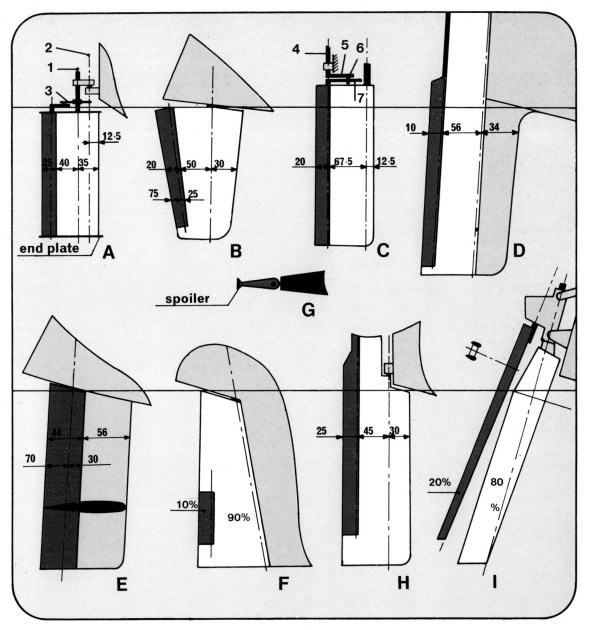

end plate   A

spoiler   G

31

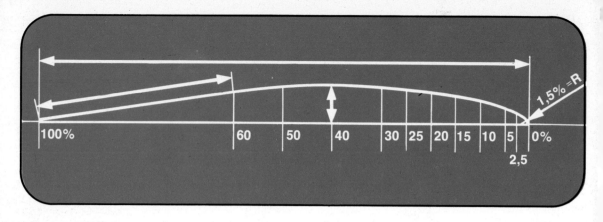

2.9. *The cross-section illustrated here is suitable for an auxiliary rudder or for a pendulum. The figures relate to a cross-section thickness that is 15 % of the chord. If a thicker blade is required for constructional reasons all the figures should be increased proportionally. The aftermost 40 % should be flat. The maximum thickness is 40 % aft from the leading edge.*

Suitable thicknesses expressed as percentages of the chord length at points aft from the leading edge (chord = 100) are:

2·5 — 2.32	30 — 7·15
5 — 3·24	40 — 7·40
10 — 4·55	50 — 7·17
15 — 5·50	60 — 6·12
20 — 6.22	100 — 0·3–0·5
25 — 6·76	

fore-and-aft axis and the rudder is the same as that between the trim tab and the rudder. This can be achieved by adjusting the size of the trim tab.

A pendulum is in fact a trim tab hung quite independently of the rudder. This makes it particularly suitable for boats with an inboard rudder stock when the fitting of a trim tab is difficult and the linkage vulnerable. A pendulum is often better than a trim tab for boats with a rudder hung at the stern too because a pendulum steering system discourages yawing more effectively than a trim tab system. An exception to this is when a trim tab is fitted to an overbalanced rudder, this being the combination that has the greatest damping effect. A pendulum is easier to replace at sea than a trim tab and it can also serve as a jury rudder if strongly enough made. Most pendulums are made in one piece but dividing them lengthwise has its attractions with a view to strength. A fixed

skeg and trim tab are then provided, such as is used by the Gunning vane gear among others (figure 5.12).

The Gunning vane gear's pendulum is actually so large that it is not easy to replace when under way. It is so solidly made that when the stern swings wildly it can be damaged by the force of the water and the resulting force of inertia. The mountings of everything at the stern are subjected to very heavy stresses and the Gunning wind vane fitted to *Robertson's Golly* was severely damaged in this way during the 1976 OSTAR.

The pendulum can also be compared to a partially balanced auxiliary rudder and, just as such rudders have about 20 % of the total area forward of the axis, the pendulum is about 20 % of the area of pendulum and rudder combined. The pendulum's profile shape is also similar to that of a rudder, and a cross-section is illustrated in figure

2.9. The force delivered can easily be varied by altering the length of the pendulum, and it is therefore possible to obtain the rudder deflection desired for a given pendulum deflection without much difficulty.

The pendulum should turn in the same direction as the rudder so that force f augments steering force F (figure 2.11). If the boat is close hauled and has definite weather helm when heeling the pendulum should cause the rudder to deflect further as wind and weather helm increase. The pendulum will swing to windward and threaten to come out of the water, and therefore must be long enough to prevent vane efficiency being affected, while weather helm must be countered by only a small degree of rudder deflection.

Linkages

The linkage which transmits vane movement via the trim tab or pendulum to the rudder is the least conspicuous part of self-steering gears but is nevertheless very important. There are innumerable possibilities, including lines, levers, push-pull cables, hydraulic systems, gear wheels etc. The vane gears described later give some examples.

Linkages can be classified in three groups:
A: Direct linkage. Deflection of the trim tab or pendulum causes uncontrolled rudder deflection and negative feedback.
B: Differential linkage. Trim tab deflection causes an appropriate deflection of the rudder. Rudder movement has positive feedback when this linkage is used.
C: Fixed linkage. Trim tab deflection is adjustable and causes an appropriate deflection of the rudder, but its rudder movement only has neutral feedback.

Direct linkage is really hardly suitable for wind vane steering gears because steering is not proportional and yawing is not countered. Fixed linkage is proportional but does not counter yawing, and trim tab deflection is independent of rudder movement. The linkage would be fixed if point P in figure 2.10A were fixed to the rudder blade. Differential linkage is the most suitable for wind vane steering gears.

Various linkages are shown in figure 2.10. The direct linkage in A has no differential, but construction is so easy that this system is popular with amateur builders. Deviation from course results in deflection a at the wind vane which in turn causes deflection b at the trim tab, as a result of which the rudder moves. As can be seen in the figure, the more the rudder deflects the greater does angle b become and, consequently, the smallest deflection of the trim tab results in an over reaction of the rudder and, with that, oversteering. The degree of alteration of course (vane deflection) is not in proportion with the degree of course correction (rudder deflection).

In $B1$ the wind vane arm's pivot is so placed that the initial trim tab deflection b reduces gradually as the rudder moves out. This is a differential linkage, and the rudder consequently achieves a state of equilibrium. For example, if the trim tab is deflected $10°$ when the rudder is amidships the rudder will react very quickly but will slow down and stop at an angle of $5°$. The trim tab will only be deflected $5°$ at this point. As the rudder deflects further the trim tab deflection decreases and the force delivered by the trim tab will consequently be too small to affect the rudder at its greater deflection. The rudder moves back again, the trim tab deflection increases, and so on until equilibrium is achieved. The result is that rudder deflection is proportional to deviation from course. The sequence described above is valid for partially balanced or unbalanced rudders. When the rudder is overbalanced as shown in $B2$ the deflection of the rudder continues until a state of equilibrium $F \times L = f \times l$ is reached, the trim tab deflection being first reduced to nil and

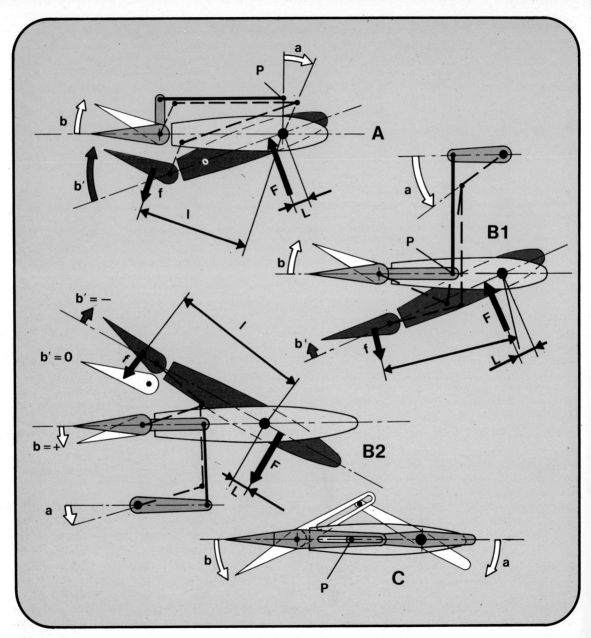

34

2.10. *Partially balanced rudders—types A to C:*

A   No differential linkage is used here. Angle b increases as rudder deflection increases. The state of equilibrium f × l = F × L cannot be achieved because the rudder deflects so far. This type of linkage can only be used if rudder movement is limited by stops or lines, or when great force is required to move the helm.

B1 Differential linkage and a partially balanced rudder. Angle b decreases as rudder deflection increases until, finally, a state of equilibrium f × l = F × L is reached.

B2 Differential linkage and an overbalanced rudder. As the rudder deflects angle b decreases and, when the rudder deflects further, the trim tab works negatively until eventually f × l = F × L is achieved.

C   The method illustrated here is often used for differential linkage. The position of pivot P determines the linkage ratio and the trim tab's effect. This acts as a differential linkage when P is aft of the rudder stock as drawn, but if P is forward of the rudder stock the linkage acts as at A.

finally becoming negative.

A linkage based on the same principle as *B* is illustrated at *C*, with the vane arm pivoting at the rudder stock. This can be attractive from the construction point of view but is by no means essential.

Differential linkage has further advantages when the trim tab is fixed in its central position. When the rudder is deflected manually the trim tab will increase the rudder's effect as shown at *D*. The boat can also be steered manually by the trim tab, and the helmsman then has to exert the minimum of effort. Yet another possibility is to use the trim tab to help balance the boat. It is then not locked centrally but set at an angle to the rudder, the deflection being such that the boat is balanced. The helmsman only has to make minor corrections by hand to keep the boat on course.

The vane can also be connected to the pendulum with or without differential linkage. When differential linkage is used as the pendulum swings sideways it is turned back towards the direction of the waterflow about its vertical axis and, consequently, the change of course is in proportion to pendulum deflection. Without differential linkage the angle of the pendulum to the centreline does not change as it swings up and this deflection is maintained until the pendulum can deliver no more turning power to the rudder. The latter system can work well when a lot of power is required to move a rudder, but over-steering will occur with partially balanced rudders because even a small deviation from course will result in large corrective rudder deflection.

Keeping the boat steady

The harmful effect yawing has on the wind vane has been mentioned already, and it is left either to the hull shape or to the steering system to discourage the boat from swinging. A large rudder helps to keep the boat steady, but only because it resists the sideways pressure of water that results from yawing. If the rudder blade yields to pressure yawing will not be countered. A rudder with a trim tab, or a pendulum with differential linkage, can

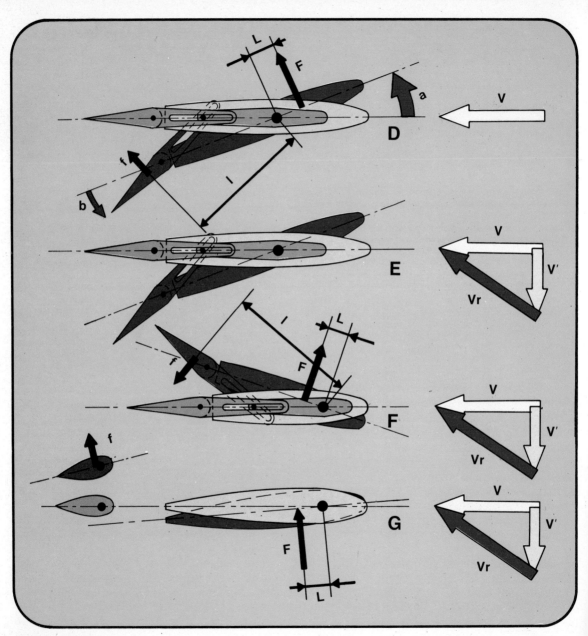

2.10. Partially balanced rudders—types D to G:

D   The deflection a of an overbalanced rudder with trim tab is opposed by the trim tab deflection b. This stabilises an overbalanced rudder and makes manual steering possible. To the helmsman it feels like a partially balanced rudder.

E   The sideways waterflow V' resulting from yawing causes an overbalanced rudder to deflect in the direction that counters the yawing motion. Vr is the resultant water force which arises from the combination of waterflow due to boat speed, V, and yawing speed V', i.e. the sideways movement of the rudder.

F   The lateral waterflow arising from yawing causes a partially balanced rudder to deflect in a direction which increases the yawing motion. Although the deflection is small it acts in the wrong sense and hinders the establishment of equilibrium $f \times 1 = F \times L$.

G   A pendulum can also deflect the rudder so that it counters yawing if the force generated by the pendulum is greater than the force needed to move the rudder when both meet the lateral waterflow. Pendulum force f acts in the same direction as rudder force F and both contribute to the total force required to steer the boat. This is also the case with the trim tabs of overbalanced rudders, but the trim tabs of balanced rudders reduce steering force.

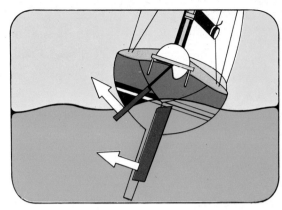

2.11. When the boat is close hauled the pendulum comes partly out of the water as she heels. Pendulum and rudder both move in the same direction and therefore both contribute to the steering force while the pendulum can also help to counter yawing. The pendulum swings up to windward on a close hauled course to counter weather helm. If it is not long enough it can come out of the water when the boat heels hard over in a gust, and will then not be able to counter the increased weather helm automatically.

help to some degree. The rudder movement caused by the lateral waterflow is then opposed immediately, and stopped by the deflection of the pendulum or the trim tab resulting from this rudder movement. The pendulum itself meets the lateral waterflow and consequently turns in such a way that a force is exerted on the rudder, moving it back against the lateral water pressure. The rudder is so deflected that it opposes the yawing movement and brings the boat back on course. Obviously a pendulum can counter yawing more effectively than a trim tab because, although the latter stops rudder movement, the rudder is left in a position where it does not correct the course. Yawing is particularly bad when rudders are actuated directly by the wind vane because the vane then has to be powerful enough to prevent the rudder

moving as a result of lateral water pressure. It is generally unable to do so and the boat diverts some way from her course before the vane makes a correction, while yawing is not countered.

The foregoing holds good for partially balanced rudders and for those with a skeg, where force F is exerted through a point aft of the rudder stock. If the rudder is overbalanced the force is exerted through a point forward of the stock. In other words, a negative force is delivered to the tiller and the rudder will swing round if the helm is left free. This combination not only does all that a normal rudder can do, but also counters yawing positively. An additional advantage is that F and f act in the same direction so that the steering power of an overbalanced rudder is $F+f$ rather than $F-f$ as with a conventional rudder with servo tab. 2·10 D shows how a trim tab stabilises an overbalanced rudder. Deflection a at the rudder causes deflection b at the trim tab. Because $f \times l$ is greater than $F \times L$ the rudder is returned to its central position, pressure on the tiller being the same as with a partially balanced rudder. When the trim tab is locked the rudder can be used for manual steering. E shows how yawing is countered. The lateral waterflow V' resulting from the yawing movement exerts force F on the rudder. As F acts through the centre of pressure forward of the rudder stock it moves the rudder until the state of equilibrium $F \times L = f \times l$ is reached. In the case shown here the boat's stern yaws to port and the rudder gives the necessary correction to starboard. With this system the vane only needs to hold the trim tab in the right position and it is the rudder itself that exerts the steering force. The vane can therefore be small but, like the linkage, must be meticulously made to channel the steering forces correctly and to avoid rudder vibration.

A positive reduction in yawing can be achieved by combining either a pendulum with a rudder or a trim tab with an overbalanced rudder. If an auxiliary rudder is fitted there is an additional advantage in that the main rudder can be fixed and will then be able to contribute to directional stability or, in other words, to keeping the boat steady by countering yawing. This, together with the sensitivity of an overbalanced auxiliary rudder and its trim tab, makes the system superior. An alternative which performs equally well is that used by Sailomat where a completely balanced auxiliary rudder is served by a pendulum instead of a trim tab. How it operates is that, when the pendulum meets a lateral waterflow, it turns the specially designed balanced auxiliary rudder to which it is matched in such a direction that yawing is reduced immediately and, because the pendulum acts in the same direction as the rudder, steering power is increased.

Course setting

Many of the mechanisms used to set the course can be seen in the illustrations. There are remote control systems which can be set, say, from the cockpit, and simple methods which can only be set at the vane itself (figure 1.11). Either a continuous or a graduated system can be used. An example of continuous setting is on a later model Hasler vane system (figure 5.9) which has a worm gear to permit very exact course setting. How

2.12 Photos A and B show the linkage of figure 2.10C in action, with the trim tab arm fixed centrally and the rudder controlled manually. Clearly the trim tab increases the effect of the rudder considerably and is forcing it back amidships.

In C the trim tab can be seen in action when it is being used as a servo-tab to actuate the rudder. The trim tab arm can be controlled by a vane, an automatic pilot or manually. Here it acts in opposition to the rudder and this is very useful at sea because the steering force required is very small indeed. The method used in figures A and C would be required when manoeuvring in harbour.

The photos show a well-constructed gear. The rudder is actuated by a wheel that is connected to it by cables and a quadrant. Heavy stops, invisible beneath the quadrant, protect the rudder when the boat is going astern etc. The rudder stock extends above the deck so that a jury tiller can easily be fitted. The trim tab arm (or tiller) pivots on the rudder stock.

D shows the layout inside the boat. The lower quadrant actuates the rudder while the smaller upper quadrant which serves the trim tab can be given a tiller to permit manual steering. The quadrant can be locked centrally by the latch in the middle of the photograph. The trim tab can also be locked when the Sharp automatic pilot is in control.

This type of system is very robust and, because very little output is required from the automatic pilot, power consumption is low. The automatic pilot can also be replaced by wind vane gear. The rudder is similar to that in figure 2.8D.

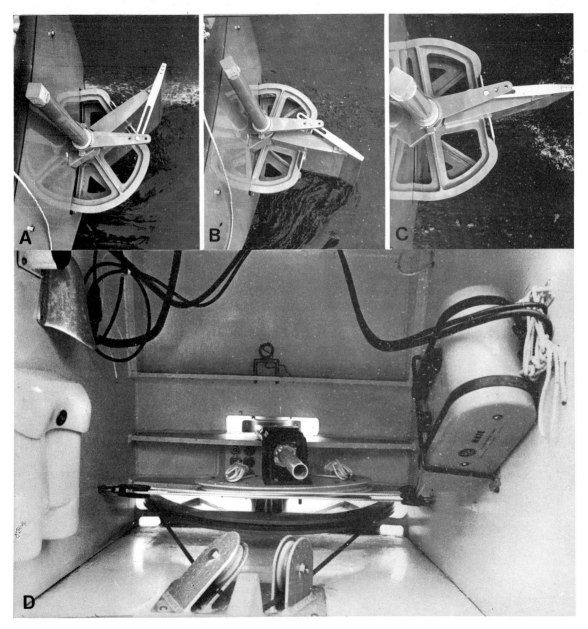

2.13. SPANIEL, *the successful Polish competitor in the 1976 OSTAR, used a home-made vane gear with two balanced rudders hung aslant. These were controlled either by an automatic pilot or by a horizontally pivoted wind vane. The windward rudder lifted out of the water as the boat heeled to a gust, but the steering force of the leeward rudder automatically increased as it became more deeply submerged, and countered the increase in weather helm resulting from heeling.*

accurately the course can be set with graduated mechanism depends on the number of stages. Figure 4.9 shows a gear wheel and latch system, but the course can be set no closer than 10° because there are 36 teeth.

A continuous setting system such as that of the Hasler vane gear can also be used to adjust the course without first having to uncouple the vane. This means less work than with a graduated system where the vane has to be uncoupled and the boat put on to her new course manually. Once she has settled the vane is recoupled and takes charge again.

3 Choosing a wind vane gear

The wind vane on board

These are the features of wind vane gears to compare: sensor, course setting, linkage, multiplication of power and steering. Appendix 1 summarises the various alternatives for each of these, and innumerable permutations are possible. There are many examples in this book, including some combinations that are better forgotten. The real question is, which vane gear to choose for which boat. It is not just the boat's behaviour that has to be considered but also the conditions in which the vane gear will be required to work. The vane gear and the boat must work together. A boat will not sail well with a poor sail plan and, equally, a boat will not steer herself well if the wrong vane gear has been selected. The shape of the stern affects the choice. If the boat has a transom-hung rudder an inexpensive gear with a trim tab can be fitted, but a yacht with an overhang aft requires a more complicated gear. There is no limit to the size of boat to which vane gears can be fitted, and appropriate systems have long been used on boats up to 20 metres in length and more.

Before selecting the wind vane gear some idea is needed of the boat's directional stability, which is her inherent ability to counter yawing. Her reactions when the rudder corrects the course, and her behaviour when the tiller is fixed, are both important. How she behaves when the helm is free does not matter because this situation does not occur while the vane is steering. For example, although a boat built to a modern design may bear away immediately when the helm is released she will be well suited to vane steering, staying more or less on course when the tiller is fixed. On the other hand a heavy boat with a long keel reacts slowly when the helm is released and her inertia can cause difficulties when the vane gear is steering. Such a boat will react too slowly when the vane corrects the course.

The hull

The type of boat best suited to vane steering gear has the following characteristics: easy to balance but with slight weather helm, not too slow to react to the helm, inherent resistance to yawing, does not accelerate suddenly as a result of going off course, only a moderate increase in weather helm when heeling to a stronger gust, and a long waterline with moderate beam.

A large rudder separate from the keel considerably augments directional stability and resists yawing. Modern boats with a relatively large rudder hung far aft and a short keel are preferable to long keel boats in this respect. Furthermore, when boat speed alters the balance is less affected if a boat has a short keel rather than a broad continuous keel. The position of the centre of the lateral resistance (CLR) in a long keel boat

3.1. *Here one hull, of a directionally stable design, is shown with a long keel above and a fin and skeg configuration below. The latter makes the greater contribution to stability, one reason being that when boat speed increases the centre of lateral resistance (CLR) moves less when the keel is short, and the boat is therefore less likely to luff up suddenly. With a long keel the CLR shifts appreciably further forward as the boat accelerates, with the result that weather helm increases considerably. A separate rudder can help to counter yawing and thus increases directional stability. The angle of incidence of the waterflow is altered when the rudder meets a lateral flow of water and a steering force arises that opposes the yawing movement. The hull's directional stability is due to the following factors.*

1.   *A long waterline combined with a narrow beam.*
2.   *Shallow forefoot.*
3.   *Slack bilges.*
4.   *Straight topsides.*
5.   *Fine lines aft.*
6.   *The buoyancy of the overhangs forward and aft is balanced so that the position of the centre of buoyancy does not shift when the boat heels.*
7.   *Moderate freeboard forward and aft.*
8.   *The centre of gravity of the boat (B) lies forward of A, the hull's centre of lateral resistance (by no means always possible).*

    Fin and skeg boats sail better to windward, are faster in light airs and are more manoeuvrable, quite apart from the greater contribution made to stability by this configuration.

    Most of the successful monohulls taking part in the OSTARs have most of the characteristics listed above, and a boat like BESTEVAER *has them all, but there are disadvantages. Due to the lack of beam there is less space for accommodation and great draught is required for stiffness. In view of the many good self-steering systems now available it is undesirable to put too much emphasis on directional stability when designing a boat for general purpose sailing because other design requirements are bound to suffer.*

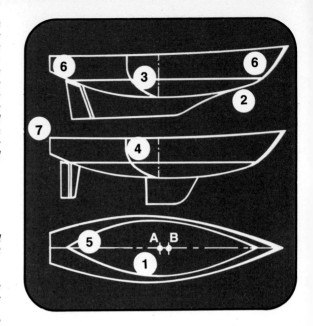

depends partly on boat speed. As speed increases the CLR shifts further forward and weather helm increases. The CLR barely moves if the boat has a short keel and, consequently, the rudder does not have to be applied to compensate for the shift in the CLR.

    The effect of the angle of heel on trim is also important when it comes to directional stability. The centre of buoyancy (CB) of the hull should shift aft as little as possible when the boat heels because when the CB moves the rudder has to compensate for the alteration in the trim of the boat. The displacement of the overhangs forward and aft, which are immersed when the boat heels, should be as similar as possible to avoid a shift in the CB.

    The type of vane gear will also be governed by the amount of force required to move the helm, a low requirement for power always being desirable. A partially balanced rudder is satisfactory in this respect, but a rudder with a skeg also has its attractions provided that the skeg area is at least 40% of the total area of rudder blade and skeg. If a rudder demands a great deal of steering force an improvement can be made for vane gear steering by using elastic strops to give the rudder some bias so that the vane only has to provide enough power

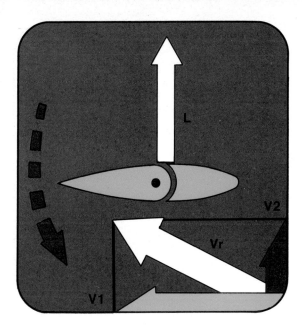

3.2. *An independently hung rudder can reduce yawing when fixed. The angle of incidence of the waterflow past the rudder alters as the stern moves sideways through the water when the boat swings. The resultant lift force (L) at the rudder thrusts the boat back on to her old course, thus countering yawing. The mizzen of a two-masted boat acts similarly. Although a long keel also steadies a boat it is less effective due to its hydrodynamically inefficient shape. Vr, resultant waterflow. V1, original waterflow. V2, waterflow due to yawing.*

for small corrections. Elastic strops can also be used on a beam reach or close hauled if the boat carries a great deal of weather helm, but this solution is not ideal because they have to be adjusted with every change of wind speed. A small degree of inherent weather helm is desirable as this increases the stability of the steering system.

The rig

The type of rig and the trim of the sails play a major part in keeping the boat steady. Sloop rig with mainsail and genoa is best purely from the point of view of speed, but with directional stability in mind there are many advantages in breaking up the sail plan longitudinally into many separate sails. For a cruising boat a compromise has to be found between directional stability and speed. Sail trimming too is something of a compromise because when sails are trimmed to keep the boat steady boat speed suffers, directional stability being improved by oversheeting the genoa and leaving the mainsail too slack. When the wind is free an extra foresail boomed out to windward contributes to directional stability.

A better answer is to set a staysail, the genoa and mainsail then being trimmed for speed and the staysail providing the directional stability desired. The staysail will be fully hardened on practically all points of sailing, and its sheet has to be led to a track because it is the athwartships position of the sheet that trims the boat. The boat can be made to luff up or to bear away without altering the helm by sheeting the staysail further inboard or outboard. A mizzen also increases directional stability. Staysail and mizzen can then be trimmed to balance the boat while the mainsail and genoa are trimmed to provide propulsion. On a run, twin headsails increase stability and ease the demands on the vane gear on this point of sailing which is particularly difficult for steering gears.

When the angle of heel increases the centre of effort of the sails (CE) shifts further to leeward and tends to cause the boat to luff up. This has a great effect on how the boat is steered, and the self-steering gear must be able to counter the increase in weather helm. A well-designed hull is a great help, and so is shortening sail at the right moment. With a low aspect ratio sail plan the CE shifts less far outboard and consquently induces less weather

43

helm than a high aspect ratio rig. Stiff boats that do not heel readily suffer less, but the fact that they will be beamy reduces their directional stability. Multihull configuration is better than a monohull in this respect because such a boat sails at only a slight angle of heel, the length to breadth ratio is extremely high, and two hulls are always immersed. On the other hand multihulls are likely to accelerate suddenly as a result of surfing or bearing away, with all the unfortunate consequences that result from steering in relation to the direction of the apparent wind.

The question of the stability of different rigs is considered more fully in chapter 8.

Determining inherent directional stability

Figure 3.3 shows various reaction patterns of boats that have gone off course These patterns can be used to describe the behaviour of boats either with the helm fixed or when the tiller is correcting the course. Few conclusions as to a boat's inherent directional stability can be drawn from studying her design. Some of the characteristics of boat and rig which affect stability have already been mentioned, but the problem is too complicated to determine a behaviour pattern in this way.

Behaviour when the helm is fixed is easy to establish, and a trial trip quickly shows into which category the boat falls on the various points of sailing. More difficult is to judge the boat's reactions when course is changed manually. It is then a question of the degree of helm that has to be applied in relation to the degree of deviation from course, ignoring any stabilising effect that may be given by a steering gear. This is how the simplest of wind vane gears and automatic pilots would steer, the boat being entirely dependent on her inherent directional stability. A simple automatic pilot can be used to determine a boat's inherent stability or,

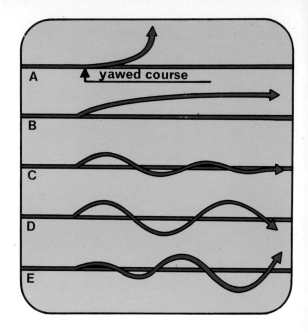

3.3.
A   Yawing is not opposed and the boat immediately deviates further from her course.
B   Yawing is opposed strongly and the boat returns to her original course.
C   Yawing is opposed positively, the swings either side of the course decrease progressively until the boat returns to her original course.
D   Neutral. Here, after going off course, the boat continues to oscillate but does not return to her original course.
E   Yawing is not opposed. She deviates from her course and continues to oscillate, the swings increasing every time. She cannot return to her original course.

3.4. *The last of Sir Francis Chichester's boats,* GIPSY MOTH V. *A staysail ketch rig like this is so versatile that good directional stability can virtually be guaranteed.*

alternatively, the working of the automatic pilot simulated using the method devised by John S. Letcher Jr. A certain compass course of, say, 40° is selected and the boat is allowed to deviate from this to, perhaps, 50°. Now try to bring the boat back on course, always applying the same degree of helm as the degree the boat has been diverted from her course. It is necessary to know exactly how far the rudder deflects, and a rudder position indicator or a protractor fitted below the tiller will give this information. One of the crew then keeps checking how far the boat deviates from her original course while the helmsman always applies a corresponding correction to the helm. The ratio between deviation from course and rudder deflection can thus be found by experiment, and the boat's behaviour and inherent directional stability can be determined by using this procedure on different points of sailing. A vane gear can then be chosen that will be appropriate for the boat, due to all the knowledge gathered about her such as steering power required, inherent directional stability, weather helm, the effect of heeling, behaviour when the helm is fixed, and so on.

Continued on page 48

3.5. *This aerial photograph of* SECOND LIFE *shows her sailing quietly over the waves, but just take a closer look and see how large the waves are.*

3.6. SECOND LIFE *under storm sails. With a broken-up sail plan a self-steering gear is not needed on a close hauled course. When the main is hoisted and the genoa replaces the storm jib the boat is still so stable that the self-steering gear barely improves her performance to windward.*

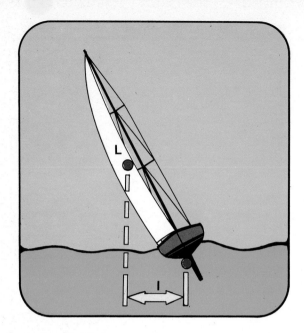

3.7. *When the boat heels the centre of effort of the resultant air force L is moved outboard and the couple L × l that arises increases as the boat heels further. It is this couple that causes weather helm to increase.*

The choice

If the boat comes into category 3.3B no wind vane is needed to steer her, but there are in fact few boats that are so well balanced on all points of sailing. If a boat is as stable as this the state of equilibrium in which she sails is linked to a specific wind strength and any change in wind speed will result in an alteration of course which will continue until equilibrium has been re-established. A wind vane can prevent these undesired deviations from course and, because it has only to deal with course corrections, the very simplest type can be used provided that the vane reacts only in proportion to the degree of deviation from course. The vane must also be powerful enough to move the rudder and to prevent undesired rudder movement caused by lateral water pressure when the stern swings. A wind vane that is not sufficiently powerful for the latter will be well able to correct the boat's course, but yawing will be accentuated.

A wind vane is also unnecessary in categories C and D provided the boat does not swing too far either side of the course, but if her behaviour with the tiller fixed falls into these categories it may well be advisable to use a wind vane to augment her inherent stability and keep oscillation to a minimum. The vane must counter yawing to some extent as well as correcting the course when the wind strength changes. If the vane actuates the main rudder it is best if the rudder is overbalanced. Should the main rudder be of conventional design best results will be obtained with a pendulum gear. A trim tab could perhaps be fitted aft of a conventional rudder if differential linkage were fitted between trim tab and rudder. The boat can also be steered by a simple combination of wind vane and auxiliary rudder when the main rudder is fixed.

Behaviour as in *A* and *E*, when the boat does not stop swinging, raises problems. The wind vane then has to react to deviations from course resulting in wind speed and also steer the boat continuously. Furthermore this vane gear must be able to make a real contribution to countering yawing and this it is able to do but only pendulum vane gears with a differential linkage, or steering gears that combine an overbalanced rudder with a trim tab, are practicable. Both systems work even better when they are fitted as auxiliary rudders while the boat is being steered by the wind vane.

The requirements set out here are severe with a view to assembling a self-steering system that is powerful enough for the more difficult points of sailing It appears in fact that only the more sophisticated gears perform well enough to achieve this aim.

Naturally a compromise can be made between the type of vane gear and the self-steering performance desired, and simple vane gears are therefore also very important. It is as well to keep an eye open for the limitations of each system, and to make no exaggerated demands or expect impossibly high performance.

Sailing area

The area in which a vane will be used affects the choice. Lower quality wind vanes can be used for short coastal passages because the vane gear is merely an aid in these waters. It is a very different matter when making long passages alone or with a small crew. The vane gear then becomes extremely important, and almost as vital as the sails themselves if the trip is to be a success.

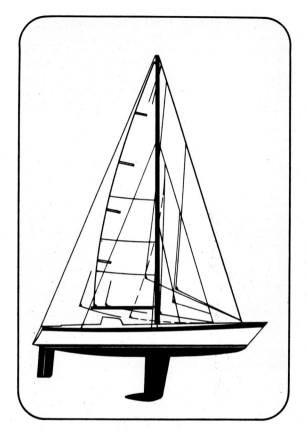

3.8. *This 16·40 metre single-handed racing boat* BESTEVAER *has a very extreme underwater body but directional stability is excellent due to the large rudder (see also figure 2.8E), the high length to breadth ratio, and the similar displacement of her overhangs forward and aft. She is very light on the helm and is therefore suitable for steering systems with a wind vane or an automatic pilot. The steering force delivered by the rudder is high although the tiller can be steered with one finger. The work required at the helm actually reduces as rudder deflection increases because the balanced part of the rudder blade forward of the axis then acts more effectively.*

4 Home construction of wind vane gears

4.1. *The QME is a simple vane gear suitable for small sailing boats that have good inherent directional stability. The vane pivots on a horizontal axis, the course is set by adjusting line 2, and the helm is actuated by tiller line 1. Due to the vane having a horizontal axis every deviation from course causes it to flap right over when the rudder is balanced. When the rudder requires a certain degree of steering power the vane leans over until the force delivered by the vane is balanced by the force on the helm. The degree of correction applied after the boat goes off course is not proportional to the degree of deviation from course. Yawing cannot be countered when the vane is directly connected to the tiller and, if the vane is not powerful enough to prevent the tiller moving when the rudder meets lateral waterflow, the boat's ability to counter yawing is adversely affected. Reasonable results can be expected when working to windward, but these systems often perform disappointingly off the wind.*

Examples

It is certainly not impossible to construct your own wind vane gear. Many cruising men have made a satisfactory device themselves and fitted it to their boats. Commercially made components are generally used for bearings etc, but most important is to have a certain amount of ingenuity. It will take some effort but you can get your boat to steer herself at little expense. Vane gear kits are also available, such as the inexpensive kit offered by Quantock Marine Enterprises (figure 4.1).

Another simple wind vane for home construction is that built by R. C. Waller for *Mani*, a small sailing cruiser just six metres in length. The wind vane steers her well although she is not steady on the helm. The details can be seen clearly in figure 4.2. The bearing is just a normal, common bearing such as that used for an electrically-driven grindstone, as found on almost every workbench. The tiller lines run direct from the drum to the helm, and must cross each other before being made fast to the tiller because, otherwise, the vane will act in reverse taking the boat further off course instead of bringing her back onto it. To operate the gear:

A   Trim the sails so that the boat is as well

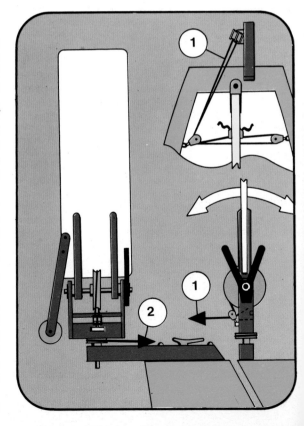

balanced as possible on the course desired.

B Allow the vane to weathercock to align itself with the wind.

C Make the tiller lines fast to the jam cleats on the tiller and . . . the boat will steer herself.

A slight adjustment may sometimes be needed to counter weather helm before she will stay exactly on course. *Mani*'s skipper noticed that, when the vane was steering in light breezes, moving the weight of his body caused her to go off course, and it appears therefore that there is a lower limit to the size of boat for which vane gears are suitable.

The wind vane sketched in figure 4.4 is the home-made self-steering gear fitted to *Stormy Weather II*. Like the Automate vane gear on which it is based it is suitable for yachts up to about three tons displacement. Again bearings for powered grindstones etc are used, the lower bearing (1) being bolted to the transom while the upper bearing (2) in which the vane pivots is attached to the guardrail. The wind vane is not fixed to the axis because it would then be impossible to set the course.

A wheel with notches sawn into it at regular intervals is welded to the axis (2). The hollow tube on which the vane is mounted is slipped over this axis and connected to the linkage mechanism by a small lever. This can be raised and, to set the course, is lowered to engage a notch in the wheel. By varying the length of the arms 3 and 4 the best linkage ratio can be found to ensure that the change in vane angle results in the appropriate change in the auxiliary rudder's angle.

Just think . . . here is a fully automatic steering system that must have cost the builder less than the price of an anchor.

I close this section with the wind vane made by James Ogg for his Bristol 27, *Essence* (figure 4.8). It is more attractive to look at than most of the home-built vanes I have seen, and is certainly not a monstrosity to hang on the transom. This vane gear reacts very quickly to changes in wind

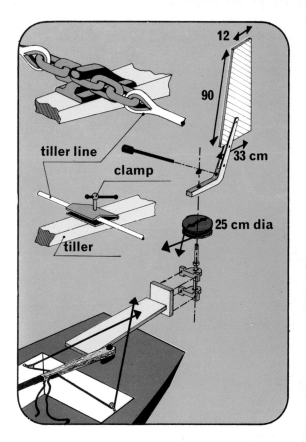

4.2. *The wind vane fitted to* MANI *is connected directly to the tiller like the QME but pivots around a vertical axis which makes construction easier than that of a horizontally pivoted vane. The tiller lines are made fast to jam cleats either side of the helm. Course setting is simpler, with a continuous tiller line made fast to a cleat on the tiller, and the tiller line must in this case be made fast to the revolving drum beneath the vane. Course setting line and tiller line are one and the same in this* MANI *system. The tiller line can also be made fast by inserting a section of chain.*

4.3. This vane gear, used by marine photographer Theo Kampa, is based on the same principle as MANI*'s and no simpler method can be imagined. The bearing is the most important component because such vanes will only work well if they can turn easily in the bearing.*

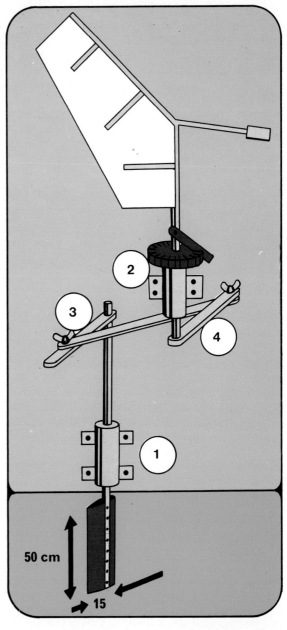

4.4. This type of wind vane, as used on board STORMY WEATHER, *is a development of the Automate vane gear. Unlike those shown so far in this chapter the vane does not drive the boat's rudder but a small auxiliary rudder. The main rudder is fixed and helps to keep the boat steady when the vane is operating. 1, bearing for the auxiliary rudder. 2, bearing for the vane, and toothed wheel for course setting. 3 and 4, linkage from vane to auxiliary rudder. The linkage ratio can be altered as desired by varying the length of the levers.*

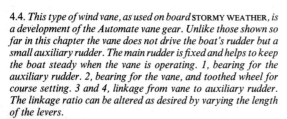

direction because, thanks to careful construction, total weight is under 10 kg while friction is kept down by using nylon bearings for all moving parts. Little friction and low weight are the two most important requirements when constructing a vane gear.

Greater vane stability is obtained by using a wedge-shaped cross-section, the vane frame being aluminium tubing over which sail cloth is stretched. The auxiliary rudder and trim tab are wooden, the axes stainless steel and the linkage aluminium. The course is set by an adjustable screw.

All the vane gears discussed here are homemade and have amply rewarded the builders for their efforts. You too can take your hands out of your pockets!

The design

The best way to decide the dimensions and the method of execution is to have a close look at whatever you see being used, or to look at the detail sketches and photographs in this book. When considering size always remember that it is not just the area of the wind vane or, say, the trim tab that is decisive but also the distance between this area and the axis about which it pivots. Multiplying this distance by the force gives the value of the turning moment delivered.

Simple wind vanes are of course the most suitable for home construction and the following systems should be considered among others.

A   Vertically pivoted vane connected directly to the tiller (cf. *Mani*). Course correction is in proportion to deviation from course provided the boat requires very little steering power. Yawing is not countered.
B   Horizontally pivoted vane connected directly to the tiller (cf. *QME*). Steering is not proportional and yawing is not countered.

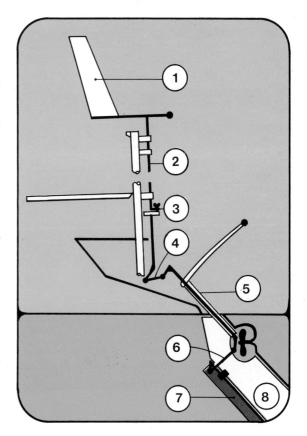

4.5. ELSELE IV*'s interesting vane gear. The vane is mounted above the mizzen where it can work in an undisturbed air stream, clear of the mizzen boom and safe from the waves. Although the linkage from vane to trim tab is not simple a solution can readily be found. No differential is incorporated here, but this would be possible if linkage such as that in figure 4.4 were used in place of the direct linkage at 4 in this figure.*

Due to the great distance between vane and trim tab it is essential to keep play, friction and the weight of all moving parts to the minimum. The mechanical linkage shown here could be replaced by a hydraulic system which would give innumerable possibilities of incorporating a differential between the vane and the trim tab. 1, vane. 2, stainless steel tube down the mizzen mast. 3, course setter. 4, direct linkage. 5, hollow rudder stock. 6, direct linkage. 7, trim tab. 8, main rudder.

4.6. *A home-made version of the Quartermaster wind vane. This is the simplest form of construction where the main rudder is served by a trim tab. The great distance between the trim tab and the rudder stock enables the trim tab to work effectively. A great deal of steering power can be produced if the trim tab is balanced. It is a pity that no differential can be incorporated with this system, which, consequently, is suitable only for boats with great inherent directional stability. Systems with the vane steering the main rudder through a trim tab are popular with amateur builders, especially when the boat has a rudder hung at the transom. Given linkage such as that shown in 4.7 performance is very reasonable.*

Although the vane is more powerful than that of A this system is still only suitable for small boats and its application is limited.

C   Vertical axis vane combined with a balanced auxiliary rudder (cf. *Stormy Weather*). Steering is proportional and the system is also suitable for larger boats. Fixing the main rudder helps to resist yawing.

D   Vertically pivoted vane actuating a trim tab on the main or auxiliary rudder (*Essence, Gaucho, Elsele*, figure 4.8). Provided a differential linkage is used between vane and trim tab this is the most successful system for home-made gears. Steering is proportional and enough power is generated for large boats. No positive reduction of yawing can be expected unless an overbalanced rudder is fitted.

Steering gears with a pendulum and an inclined axis vane are beyond the scope of most amateur builders, but they generally perform better than the systems described in A to D.

The auxiliary rudder

An auxiliary rudder is between one third and one quarter the size of the main rudder, and should be positioned at least 10% of the LWL aft of the main rudder if it is to function well. It should be balanced, with 12–20% of the rudder area forward of the axis. Drawing 2.8 gives some idea of the sizes and shapes of auxiliary rudders and/or trim tabs, and a profile shape suitable for a rudder blade can be found in fig. 2.9. The auxiliary rudder should not be lifted partly out of the water when the boat pitches if construction similar to figure 2.8A is chosen.

Once the dimensions of the trim tab or rudder have been decided it is best to make and fit them, and then take the boat out for a sail. Steering her manually through the trim tab or auxiliary rudder during this trial trip enables you to check how well they work, and to get some idea of the power the vane will have to produce. The trim tab area is correct when the angle between the rudder and the boat's centreline is virtually the same as the angle between the trim tab and the rudder. In other words, when the rudder is deflected 10° the trim tab must also deflect 10°.

The vane

There are no restrictions to the area of the wind vane. If it steers well in force 2 winds the same vane will serve at wind force 8. The reverse does not apply because a vane area that is right for wind force 8 does not produce enough power for wind force 2. In practice the deciding factor is the way the vane is constructed. It must be large enough to steer the boat in force 2 winds but strong enough to withstand a storm. This strength should not be allied to excessive weight which would all too soon lead to oversteering. From the point of view of construction it may be advisable to carry a storm vane on board, although this is not really necessary from the aspect of vane performance. Obviously the smaller size of the inclined axis vane is an advantage in this respect but they are more difficult to make. A vane connected directly to the tiller must be powerful enough to hold the helm steady against lateral waterflow such as arises when the stern yaws, or due to wave action. A vane that is not sufficiently powerful to oppose these forces cannot perform efficiently. Drawing 2.3 shows some of the vane shapes that can be used. The best angle for an inclined axis vane is between 5° and 15° to the horizontal. The linkage ratio from vane to trim tab or (auxiliary) rudder is either 1:1 or 2:1. That is to say, the trim tab or rudder will be deflected one degree when the boat goes one degree off course in the former case, but deflected two degrees in the latter case. The axis

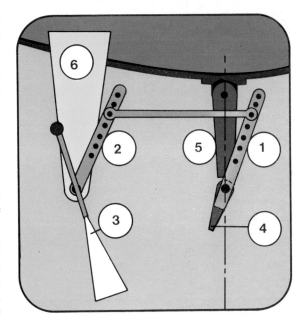

4.7. *This is probably the simplest differential linkage. 1, adjustable trim tab arm. 2, wind vane arm which can also be adjusted. 3, wind vane. 4, trim tab. 5, rudder. 6, wind vane bracket.*

about which the inclined axis vane pivots is determined by the formula given in chapter 2 which relates deviation from course to the rotation of the wind vane axis. If a vertically pivoted vane is used the degree of deviation from the course can be adjusted to the rotation of the wind vane axis, but when a vane has a horizontal axis there is no relationship between deviation from course and the wind vane's position.

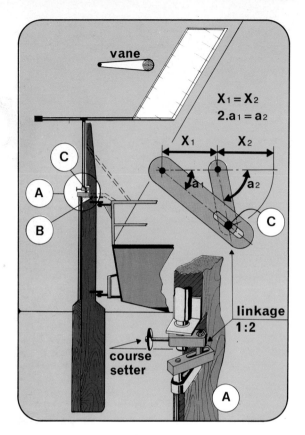

$$X_1 = X_2$$
$$2.a_1 = a_2$$

4.8. *The wind vane fitted to* ESSENCE *does not comply with linkage rule 7. It is easy to make an improvement if necessary because of the linkage mechanism incorporated (A). Here it merely provides a linkage ratio of 1:2 between vane and trim tab. All that is required to provide a differential linkage is to saw through the rudder blade at B. The upper part of the rudder blade, on which the vane pivot is mounted, would then be fixed to the boat by a bracket as indicated by the broken lines, and the system would then comply with the requirements of linkage rule 7. Rudder deflection can be increased or decreased as desired to match a given wind vane deflection. Figures 2.8C and 2.10 show similar linkages.*

Course setting

It is better to be able to set the course with infinite variation of adjustment, such as with a cleated line or a worm gear on the vane axis, rather than to be limited to particular settings. For example, when a gear wheel and lever is used the course settings possible are limited by the number of gear teeth, and with 36 teeth the boat can only be steered on courses varying by 10°.

Linkage rules

The following rules are important when linking the vane to the rudder or auxiliary rudder, and when power is augmented by a pendulum or trim tab:

1 The vane turns in the opposite direction to the auxiliary or main rudder.

2 The vane turns the opposite way to the direction in which the boat deviates from her course.

3 The vane turns in the same direction as the trim tab on the rudder.

4 A trim tab turns in the opposite direction to the rudder (with an overbalanced rudder the trim tab eventually takes up the same direction as the rudder).

5 Pendulum and rudder turn in the same direction.

6 All movements should be proportional; in other words the vane, trim tab or pendulum should deflect to a specific degree for a given degree of rudder deflection.

7 When the vane is fixed, pendulum or trim tab movement must be in a direction that opposes rudder movement. Thus when the vane is fixed the trim tab turns in the same direction as the rudder.

Rules 1 to 4 are valid for all vane gears, but this is not the case with rules 5 to 7. Many examples can be given of vane gears that do not comply with the latter, and these systems can really only be fitted to boats with great inherent directional stability. Gears that comply with rules 5 to 7 always perform noticeably better, especially when the wind is free.

It is only sensible to find out whether it will be possible for your boat to be steered by a certain method before starting to construct your own self-steering system. If she can only be controlled by a pendulum or an overbalanced auxiliary rudder it is not worth taking the trouble to make a simpler system which would not perform satisfactorily.

Unstable systems

Among the innumerable permutations of wind vane, trim tab, auxiliary rudder and so on there are some systems that are better avoided if you have doubts about the self-steering ability of your boat. The following combinations and/or principles are less suitable.

1 A horizontally pivoted wind vane (not to be confused with an inclined axis vane) especially when combined with a balanced rudder or auxiliary rudder.
2 A vane, mounted on the rudder or auxiliary rudder, which actuates a trim tab. This does not comply with linkage rules 5–7 and is illustrated in 4.8 and 1.10.
3 A powerful wind vane acting on a trim tab or pendulum with no differential in the linkage between the vane and the trim tab or pendulum. This combination complies even less with linkage rules 5–7.

Problems in use

Even when the wind vane gear has been chosen with care good performance is not guaran-

4.9. *The course setter and linkage mechanism of a home-made vertically pivoted wind vane with pendulum.*

teed. Quite apart from the effects of changes in boat speed on the course steered by the vane gear it may be inefficient, correct the course unsatisfactorily or cause oversteering. If the boat is not brought back to her original course the vane is not powerful enough. This may be due to friction, to fitting too small a wind vane and/or the multiplication of power by the trim tab or pendulum may be insufficient. This is easy to recognise and remedy.

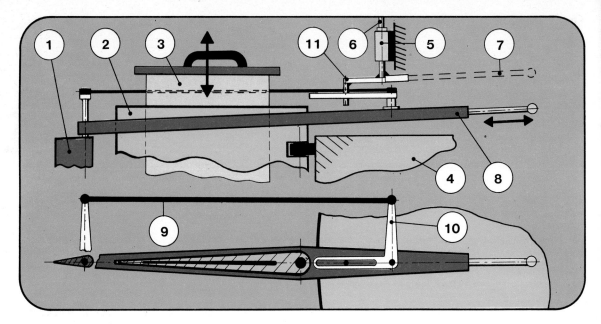

4.10. *It can be difficult to incorporate a differential linkage to a trim tab on the rudder because the actuating levers of such a linkage cross the rudder blade (or its extension). Multihulls with lifting rudders suffer from this problem, but it can be solved by using a linkage such as that shown here.*

Key:
1, Trim tab. 2, Rudder. 3, Lifting dagger-type rudder. 4, Stern. 5, Vane pivot bearing, bolted to the boat. 6, Vane pivot. 7, Removable trim tab tiller to enable the rudder to be steered manually by the trim tab. 8, Extendable tiller. 9, Push-pull rod to the trim tab. 10, Trim tab arm which pivots about a pin attached to the tiller. 11, Connection between the vane and the trim tab arm.

Oversteering

Oversteering describes the reactions of a boat being steered by a vane as shown in figure 3.3D. She responds to a course correction but shoots past her correct course and then oscillates back and forth about her course to a greater or lesser degree. This oscillation can be quick or slow and can take her a long way or less far from her course. Swinging about like this can be so extreme that she has to sail a considerably longer distance to get from *A* to *B*, while her sails will be badly trimmed half the time and comfort on board is reduced.

Oversteering is caused by:

A *Friction*
Friction causes steering gear to work too sluggishly and course corrections are transmitted too late. The boat is far off course before the correction starts to take effect and, when it does, so much helm is applied that the boat shoots past her proper course. The solution is to improve the bearings.

B *Play*
Play in the linkage mechanism has just the same effect as excessive friction and care must be taken to reduce it to a minimum.

C *Inertia*
The inertia of the moving parts of steering gear causes a definite delay in reaction to changes in wind and course, the weight of the vane and its counterpoise being particularly important. The inertia of the mass of the boat herself plays a major role and the boat does not react immediately to a course correction. It is some time before she even starts to change course and, equally, before she stops swinging when the correction is no longer being applied. It can happen that vane movements (oscillation) coincide with the boat's yawing (oscillation), and vane corrections will then be in phase with the boat as she yaws, resulting in a serious form of oversteering. One solution is to reduce the weight of the vane and/or moving parts of the linkage. A temporary solution can be to attach a piece of elastic either side of the tiller to delay rudder movement.

If neither method stops oversteering the type of wind vane used is unsuitable for the boat because her directional stability is probably inadequate to stop her oscillating. A steering system is then required that can contribute to preventing yawing, and this means a system that has a positive countering effect, such as those with a pendulum or an overbalanced rudder with trim tab. Steering must also be adjusted so that it is proportional, if this is not already the case, so that the degree of deviation from course is related to the degree of course correction applied. The differential linkage must be checked to see that the linkage rules have been observed.

Should it be impossible to replace the vane gear with one that counters yawing more effectively or provides proportional steering, oversteering may be kept within bounds by checking the tiller with two pieces of elastic as already described, or by limiting tiller movement with a stop either side.

A reduction in vane area and, consequently, in the vane efficiency can reduce oversteering, but this is not an ideal solution. With good vane gears there is really no need to fear oversteering.

5 Some commercial vane gears

Introduction

The preceding chapters looked at the demands made on vane gears and considered what can be expected from the various types. This chapter gives examples of some of the systems on the market. Many combinations are possible and, from the examples given here, it appears that there is no want of variety. A vane gear can cost from the price of a better automatic pilot to as little as one twentieth of this. Obviously better performance can be expected from a more expensive vane gear than from cheaper models.

Vane gears with an auxiliary rudder

This section includes some of the most sophisticated vane gears which employ an over-balanced rudder with trim tab or a pendulum. There are also very simple systems such as those already mentioned in chapters 1 and 4, the Automate vane gear, *Stormy Weather* and *Essence* being examples. The fact that the main rudder is fixed means that it contributes to directional stability and, should the main rudder be damaged, a complete spare rudder is provided by the vane gear. In the simpler systems the auxiliary rudder is actuated directly by the vane, whereas in the more sophisticated systems a trim tab or even a pendulum are used for this purpose. Yawing is countered if an overbalanced rudder is used, but damping is less evident with conventional auxiliary rudders.

MNOP (French)

This vane gear was designed by one of the pioneers in this field, the French aircraft engineer Marcel Gianoli. MNOP is the latest product of a long series of experiments that started with self-steering gears such as those used for the 1964 OSTAR when Jean Lacombe and Eric Tabarly both used Gianoli vane gears, although of very different designs. Eric Tabarly's series of *Pen Duick*s were notable guinea pigs for vane gears, each new *Pen Duick* being fitted with the latest improvement. After *Pen Duick II* came the enormous vane designed especially for *Pen Duick IV* and, finally, the Regall vane gear perfected for *Pen Duick V* which is now on sale although extremely expensive.

How it operates: The MNOP is disconnected for manual steering with the vane locked upright on the turret but free to weathercock in the wind. The shaft to which the auxiliary rudder (also locked) is attached is free to turn in the water and consequently offers the minimum of resistance. The axis about which the auxiliary rudder cum trim tab pivots is so far forward that behaviour is like a partially balanced rudder. To put the gear into operation:

A   Trim the sails to the course desired and fix the tiller.

B Lock the shaft with the rudder blade aligned with the waterflow so that the water exerts no lateral pressure.

C Release the auxiliary rudder (latch 9 in figure 5.1) and a stabilising effect will be exerted on the course because the trim tab is being held steady by the wind vane.

D Engage the latch in the turret (10) which the wind vane will have turned as it aligned itself with the wind. The line that engages the latch also releases lever (11) allowing the vane to turn about its inclined axis and to actuate the trim tab. The self-steering gear now takes over and your hands are free for other jobs.

When fitting the MNOP gear the auxiliary rudder must be far enough away from the main rudder (at least 10 % of the LWL) if it is to operate efficiently. The turbulence caused by the main rudder affects the performance of the auxiliary rudder if they are too close together. Should the vane gear be mounted well aft of the transom take care that the auxiliary rudder cannot come clear of the water when the boat pitches.

The standard MNOP wind vane is available in only one size and is suitable for boats up to 13 metres LOA. With larger boats there is too great a risk of the rudder coming partly out of the water when the boat pitches as she works to windward.

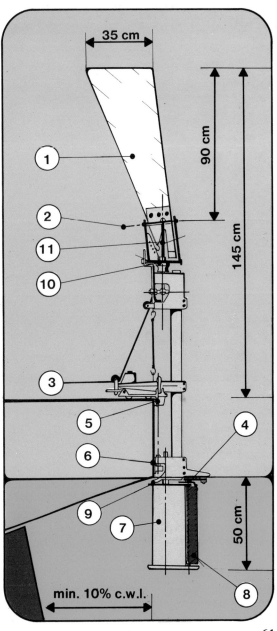

5.1. The principle of the MNOP vane gear.
1, vane. 2, wind vane axis (inclined 6·5°). 3, control line for turret latch (10) or linkage pivot (11). 4, trim tab control with differential linkage. 5, upper bracket and lock for the shaft pivot. 6, lower bracket for shaft pivot, and latch (9). When this is engaged the auxiliary rudder (7) pivots about this axis and becomes balanced instead of overbalanced. 8, trim tab. 9, latch, auxiliary rudder to shaft. 10, rotating vane turret with which the latch engages or the course is set. 11, push-pull rod, a link between vane and trim tab.

5.2. *The Mustafà wind vane gear. This is a good quality gear, largely made of aluminium, and is offered in three sizes suitable for boats varying from very small to large.*

1 The vane rotates on an axis that is almost horizontal, and a small deviation from course causes considerable vane deflection. This deflection is proportional to the degree of deviation from course due to the inclined axis.

2 Rotating head on which the vane is mounted and with which the course is set.

3 The rotating head is controlled by worm gear and fine course setting by remote control is therefore possible. The worm gear can be disengaged, leaving the vane free to turn to the wind when not operated.

4 Linkage between wind vane and the servo-rudder. The linkage ratio governing the relationship between vane deflection and servo-rudder can be adjusted.

5 Tiller that can be fixed in three positions:

A When the tiller is vertical servo-rudder and rudder are locked amidships but the vane is free to weathercock in the wind.

B When the tiller is at an oblique angle the vane gear operates.

C When the tiller is horizontal the rudder acts as a normal rudder steered manually. This rudder has the following attributes:
—The overbalanced rudder is balanced by the servo-rudder and consequently the power required for steering is very small (and remains positive).

—When the rudder moves the servo-rudder moves in the same direction, and the profile shape becomes asymmetric resulting in high lift force even at small angles of incidence. Great steering power can be delivered while resistance is kept to a minimum.

6 Fins that can be used as a ladder.

7 Servo-rudder.

8 The main rudder which corrects the course is actuated as follows:

A The rudder is moved as a result of a correction in course transmitted from the vane via the servo-rudder.

B The rudder reacts independently of the vane and, for this reason, is superior to the conventional balanced rudder. When a wave shifts the stern to one side the angle of incidence of the waterflow on the rudder alters, and this alteration is felt by the overbalanced rudder and servo-rudder. The system reacts in such a way that the boat is returned to its former course. This reaction is quick and powerful, as is essential when sailing off the wind. A and B act both independently and together.

A feels the alteration in wind direction and makes an immediate correction.

B detects small variations in the direction of the waterflow and keeps the boat steady.

C The rudder can also be steered directly by the tiller as described in point 5C.

The way the MNOP and Mustafà overbalanced rudders work is described in detail in the caption to figure 2.10.

Mustafà (Italian)

The Italian competitors in the 1976 OSTAR were almost all fitted with the new Mustafà vane gear. 'The gear has clearly demonstrated to have the capacity to steer for hours under spinnaker, both when the wind is light and the boat is barely reaching three knots and when the wind is at 25 knots.' This was the claim made by the manufacturers before the start and was confirmed by the competitors at the finish. The system is that which gives greatest directional stability, an inclined axis vane being coupled to an overbalanced auxiliary rudder with servo-rudder, and the characteristics are the same as those mentioned in connection with **MNOP** vane gears. The advantages of this

type of vane gear can be summed up as follows:

— Extreme sensitivity in light winds.

— Extreme sensitivity to small alterations in apparent wind direction.

— Very rapid reaction to a deviation from course. It is true that whereas a helmsman can anticipate major deviations from course and can adjust the boat's course to individual waves, a vane gear cannot possibly do either but, on the other hand, a wind vane never loses concentration and is therefore never taken by surprise with the boat a long way off course. This makes up for the inability to anticipate.

— Very great corrective power due to a rudder

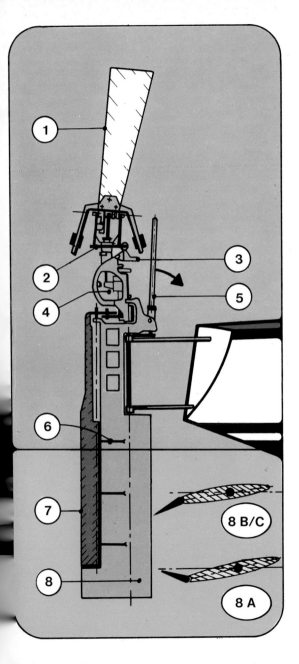

profile shape that develops a high lift force even at small angles of incidence.

Differential linkage is used between servo-rudder, vane and rudder (as explained in chapter 2). This, together with the over-balanced rudder, makes the gear sensitive to even a very slight deviation from course. The overbalanced rudder feels an alteration in the direction of waterflow much sooner than the vane recognises an alteration in wind direction. Considerable deviation from course is necessary before the vane reacts.

Although the MNOP vane gear was the first to use an overbalanced rudder to achieve the performance just described it is Mustafà that enables this type of vane gear to be used widely because it is made in three sizes and can be fitted to boats up to 18 metres LOA. The price is on the high side but, as the gear can also be used as the main rudder, this objection is countered by the fact that there need be no expenditure on a main rudder. All Mustafà vane gears have a tiller and can therefore be used immediately as main or auxiliary rudders. The way the gear works is very similar to the MNOP except that the Mustafà is locked amidships when not operating while the auxiliary rudder is free to turn in the water like the MNOP.

Sailomat (Swedish)

The Sailomat vane gear is the Swedish answer to the self-steering problem. The whole apparatus is both handsome and soundly constructed—in fact it is one of the best looking vane gears available. It operates in the same way as the MNOP and Mustafà gears except that a pendulum is used in place of trim tabs. The rudder is partially balanced, but this alters as the rudder becomes further immersed and when it is completely submerged it is fully balanced. The Sailomat's performance is very similar to that of the two preceding systems.

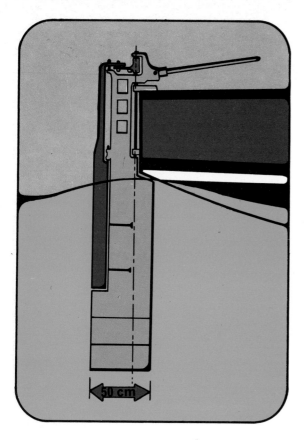

5.3. *The Mustafà vane gear's rudder can also be fitted as the main rudder and it is the height of the stern wave, as shown here, that must be taken as the level to which the rudder is immersed. All those parts of the rudder that cause great resistance should lie above the stern wave.*

Much attention is paid to technical details, roller bearings being used for the auxiliary rudder, and the pendulum being made in 'tandem'. The two blades are connected transversely, making this vulnerable component very rigid. Both pendulum and rudder can be unshipped by hand and easily brought aboard. They are also attached with shear bolts so that if the load becomes excessive, perhaps due to hitting some floating timber, the bolts will shear while the components remain intact. The entire assembly weighs barely 30 kg and is available in different sizes. If required the pendulum can be controlled by a small servo motor instead of the wind vane, and the Sailomat can then be used as an automatic pilot and will follow a compass course. The Sailomat costs about twice as much as pendulum vane gears, but when paying this you have also bought a second rudder.

RVG (USA) see fig. 5.7
The RVG vane gear has a vertically pivoted vane which actuates the rudder blade through a trim tab. The rudder is hung aft of a skeg to increase strength. The RVG vane gear is robust, with few components and simple linkage. Performance is reasonable, but this type of vane is unable to counter yawing as do the preceding wind vane gears. On the other hand RVG vane gears are only half the price and repairs are less difficult due to the simple construction.

Both vane and trim tab are wedge-shaped to speed up the gear's reaction to any deviation from course. The RVG vane gear operates as follows:

1 Put the boat on course and lock the tiller in a position where any weather helm is neutralised by the main rudder.
2 Wait until the vane, which is free to weathercock in the wind, adjusts to the new course before coupling the vane to the linkage mechanism.
3 A finer adjustment to the course can be made by turning the vane to the desired direction

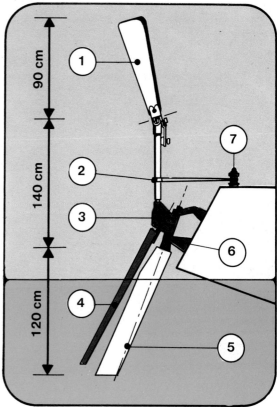

5.4. *The Sailomat vane gear fitted to this boat combines a balanced auxiliary rudder with an inclined axis vane and a pendulum. The Sailomat is one of the most advanced vane gears available. Construction is sound but without harming the appearance. The pendulum can be actuated either by a vane or by a small drive motor when it acts as an automatic pilot with very low power consumption.*

5.5. *Sailomat components.*
1, inclined axis vane. 2, course setting drum. 3, differential linkage from vane to pendulum to rudder. 4, pendulum which can turn freely in the water to avoid damage when the wind vane is not operating. 5, rudder. When fully submerged the rudder is overbalanced but the overbalance reduces progressively the higher the rudder is mounted. Originally the rudder was also produced in 'tandem' but in later models these were replaced by a single rudder blade. 6, mounting bracket. 7, remote control for adjusting course setting.
· *The entire installation weighs barely 30 kg and is available in three sizes. The Sailomat's weak point is under engine at speeds above 6 knots when it can vibrate excessively. A solution is possible by improving the method of fixing the rudder in these circumstances. Performance under sail is absolutely faultless.*

with the worm gear.

When manual steering is resumed the vane merely has to be uncoupled from the linkage. In emergencies the main rudder is, of course, powerful enough to override the vane and the course can be altered before uncoupling the vane. Auxiliary rudder systems are generally mounted on the centreline, but if this is quite impossible there is no reason why the auxiliary rudder should not be fitted to one side of the transom.

Hydrovane (UK)

The Hydrovane vane gear is composed of a horizontally pivoted vane and a partially balanced auxiliary rudder. This system can cause oversteering and, when the boat alters course, the vane does not make a correction in proportion to the degree of deviation from course. It always tries to flap right over whenever the boat goes off course. A stable system that can steer the boat reasonably well can be achieved if the sizes of the vane and auxiliary rudder are mutually appropriate, and provided the linkage between vane and auxiliary rudder is adjustable. Such systems really rely on the boat's own ability to counter oversteering.

The Hydrovane is a strong, well-made gear and considerable thought has been given to its appearance.

5.6. *The Hydrovane is a pleasant looking vane gear with horizontally pivoted vane and auxiliary rudder, but is only suitable for boats with reasonable directional stability. It is a reliable unit for boats up to about 12 metres LOA.*

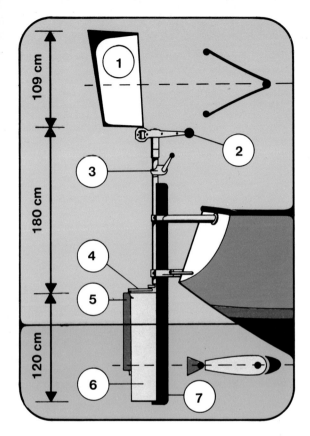

5.7. *The RVG vane gear employs a vertically pivoted vane and a fixed skeg with auxiliary rudder and trim tab. 1, wedge-shaped vane. 2, counterpoise. 3, coupling of vane to pivot. When the vane has been coupled to the linkage mechanism fine alterations to the course can be made with the worm gear. 4, linkage from vane to trim tab. 5, wedge-shaped trim tab. 6, rudder. 7, fixed skeg.*

The RVG vane gear is robust, and suitable both for very large, heavy boats (18 m LOA, 30 tons displacement) and for small boats (e.g. 8 m LOA, 6 tons displacement).

Windpilot (German)

This vane gear consists of a vertically pivoted vane which drives a balanced auxiliary rudder through two meshing gear wheels. This is one of the simplest of the systems that employs an auxiliary rudder. Thanks to the vertically pivoted vane course correction is proportional to the degree of deviation from course, which gives it an advantage over the Hydrovane, but the latter has a smaller vane. The Windpilot's vane has a stainless steel tubular frame covered with sail cloth, and is therefore very light. This vane gear is available in different sizes, and Windpilot also make a wind vane that drives the main rudder direct. Windpilot pendulum vane gear is available for boats which make high demands on vane gear, and this too has a vertically pivoted vane.

Pendulum vane gears

Pendulum vane gears are the most popular. They are very powerful, course correction is proportional to the degree of deviation from course, and they can counter yawing. Pendulum gears are easy to install and repairs can be avoided because they are easy to maintain. They cost round about £500 although considerably more expensive gears can be bought.

Continued on page 70

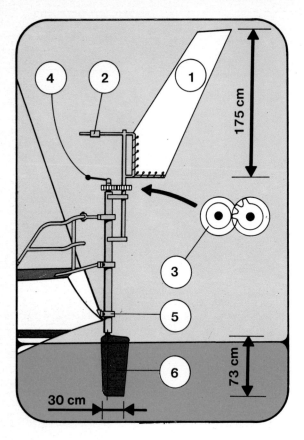

5.8. *This Windpilot vane gear is the model with vertically pivoted vane and auxiliary rudder. The vane is linked to the auxiliary rudder by two plastic gear wheels. The vane consists of a tubular frame covered with sail cloth. There are two sizes, the larger being suitable for boats displacing a maximum of 6 tons. Windpilot also produce pendulum vane gear, and a vane directly connected to the tiller. The components are:*
1, vertically pivoted vane. 2, counterpoise. 3, gear wheel linkage. 4, clamp which connects the vane to the auxiliary rudder as well as setting the course. 5, auxiliary rudder bearing. 6, balanced auxiliary rudder.

5.9. *The Hasler vane gear. 1, tiller lines made fast to a jam cleat on the helm. 2, worm gear control line which sets the course. 3, line which couples and uncouples the vane. Pulling this line disengages the worm (12) from the gear wheel (11) and the vane is free to weathercock in the wind. 4, this line locks the pendulum when the boat is under way. 5, the pendulum can be pulled out of the water with this line. 6, balanced pendulum. 7, vertically pivoted vane. 8, vane pivot. 9, pendulum's horizontal axis. 10, pendulum's vertical axis. Rudder and pendulum turn in the same direction, and pendulum lift* f *augments rudder force* F.

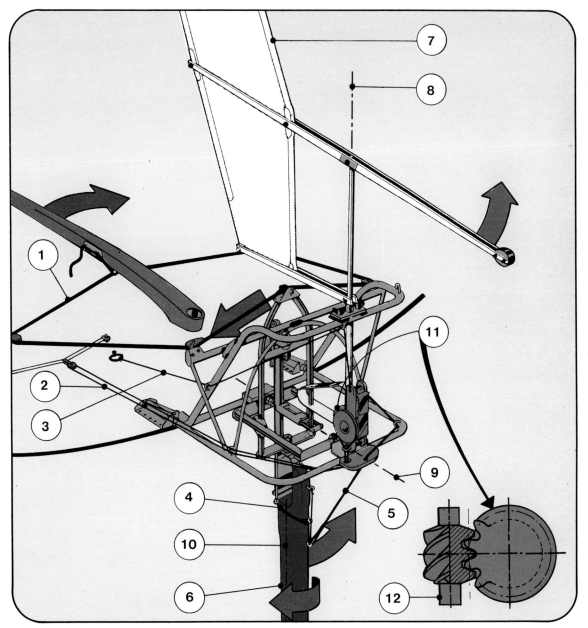

69

Hasler (UK)

The Hasler vane gear is one of the most widely used. This is due largely to the successes gained in the Observer Single-handed Trans-Atlantic Races, and to Sir Francis Chichester's and Sir Alec Rose's circumnavigations. The gear is made in three sizes for small, medium and large boats, so there is a Hasler vane gear to suit all sizes of boat. It is the displacement rather than the dimensions of the boat that decide which size should be used. The vane can also be linked to a trim tab instead of a pendulum, although the Hasler gear is not so well suited to this system. You can see that Hasler caters for almost the entire market.

The principle is familiar: the vane actuates the pendulum, the pendulum actuates the rudder, and the rudder steers the boat. The manufacturers, Gibb, have not changed this principle for years and have concentrated exclusively on improving

5.10. *The Hasler vane gear fitted to Mike McMullen's trimaran* THREE CHEERS *at the start of the 1976 OSTAR. The pendulum is suspended normally aft but, because of the low mizzen boom, the vane is fitted on one side. Two vanes are required therefore, and it is always the windward vane that is engaged. Both vanes can be used for downwind work. A better solution would have been to use one vane mounted on top of the short mizzen mast.*

construction. The results can be seen in the perfected models now available. Particular care has been taken over friction and the weight of the individual components. Both are very low and performance benefits greatly.

A change to using horizontally pivoted vanes is unlikely because current vanes appear to deliver adequate power, and the construction of these conventional vanes can be kept very simple.

No one can say that operation is difficult. Once the boat is on course the vane is set to work by releasing the line (3) so that the worm (12) engages the gear wheel (11). If a minor correction is required to get the boat right on course, perhaps to compensate for weather helm, the vane can be adjusted by using line (2) to turn the worm gear. This line can also be used to alter course, and there is no need to uncouple and reset the vane. The Hasler vane gear's vulnerability is a disadvantage, and for a long voyage it is certainly necessary to take a complete reserve unit. Chay Blyth, in particular, discovered this when a following sea buckled the framework and he had to complete his circumnavigation without a vane gear. Although he had taken spares for all the components, such as vane and pendulum, he did not have a reserve stainless steel tubular frame on which to mount

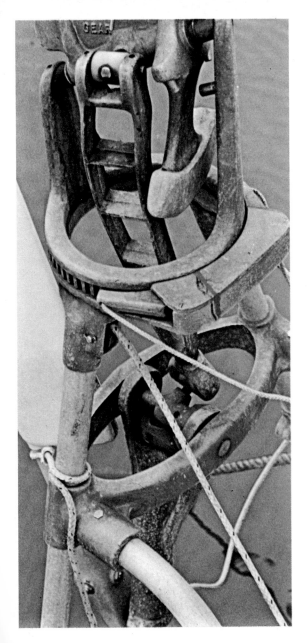

them. The Hasler gear is rather large due to the use of a vertically pivoted vane, and the linkage from the pendulum is not proportional. In other words, the pendulum stays deflected while it is swinging out. The vane is well able to deal with all the demands that can be made on this type and, in emergencies, the boat can be steered by the pendulum, for example if the rudder is fouled.

Aries (UK)

The Aries vane gear works on the same principle as the Hasler but its construction is as different as chalk from cheese. Castings, crown wheels and so on replace light rods, lines and tubes. An inclined axis vane is used which is much smaller than the vertically pivoted Hasler vane. It therefore looks more attractive and, being small, the vane is also less liable to break. Strength is the main consideration with the Aries vane gear. The model shown here is the third completely new type to be marketed and this points to the efficiency of this original system. The way to operate the gear is as follows:

1 Lower the servo paddle into the water.
2 Settle the boat on course.
3 Set the vane vertically with the course setting snaffle line.

5.11. *The Aries vane gear with inclined axis vane and pendulum (servo-paddle). Technically this is a well-constructed vane gear, with reliability the most important consideration. Unlike most systems the steering lines lead beneath the pendulum's axis of rotation and consequently have to be crossed before being made fast to the helm. They are led internally through the casting on which the vane head etc are mounted. In harbour, and when not in use, the vane is removed and the pendulum lifted 180° out of the water. Two pawls are used to adjust the vane angle to the course and the vane can be turned clockwise or counterclockwise. Like all systems that use pawls an infinite adjustment of course is impossible.*

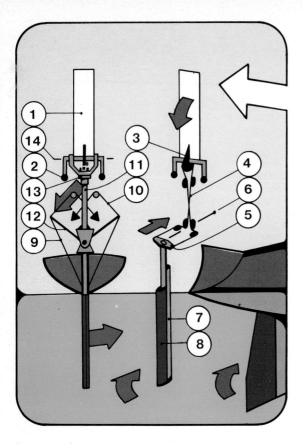

5.12. *The Gunning vane gear. 1, vane. The size for a boat displacing 13 tons is 120 × 30 cm. The vane is made of a single piece of solid ¼″ plywood. 2, counterpoise. 3, vane quadrant. 4, wires that connect the vane to the trim tab. 5, trim tab quadrant. 6, pendulum's horizontal axis. 7, skeg. 8, trim tab, the movable part of the skeg. Skeg and trim tab together form the pendulum which measures 100 × 20 cm. 9, stays. 10, tiller lines. 11, shaft or 'mast'. 12, spreaders. 13, fitting on which the vane is turned about its vertical axis as required for course setting. 14, vane's horizontal axis.*

4 Once the vane is vertical make the tiller lines fast to the helm. The system can also be coupled to wheel steering gear.

5 The boat's weather helm (pressure on the rudder) must be balanced by the steering force (pressure on the servo paddle) if the gear is to perform well. This is done by giving the tiller some bias to port or starboard, as necessary, before making the tiller lines fast.

6 Check that the vane is as nearly vertical as possible when it is operating.

7 For manual steering uncleat the tiller lines from the helm and the servo paddle will then be free to turn with the waterflow astern.

Gunning (UK)

This was designed by M. F. Gunning, a Dutchman resident in England. Deliberately omitting certain refinements, Mr. Gunning considered that setting the horizontal axis of the vane out of plumb or using differential linkage between vane and trim tab was unnecessary because the boat herself would provide the necessary stability. If your boat is capable of this there is no good reason for using a more complicated system.

A remarkable performance by this vane gear was when it brought Jerry Cartwright, a competitor in the single-handed race from San Francisco to Tokyo, safely to Hawaii. Nothing remarkable in that—apart from the fact that Jerry had a fractured skull and was lying semi-conscious in the cabin. Disaster was avoided because his vane gear was so simple to operate.

'The pendulum is split into a fixed skeg and a rear part which can be turned, the trim tab, the two forming an aerofoil section. Stays are attached to the skeg, supporting it at waterline level. The stays double as tiller lines and are led over ordinary spreaders, giving great leverage, with corresponding reduction in forces in the tiller lines. The connection of the vane to the pendulum consists of two thin wires led over a quadrant on the vane

5.13. WILD ROCKET *at full speed at the start of the 1972 OSTAR.*
This boat is one of the many French participants in single-handed
races to be fitted with the Atoms vane gear.

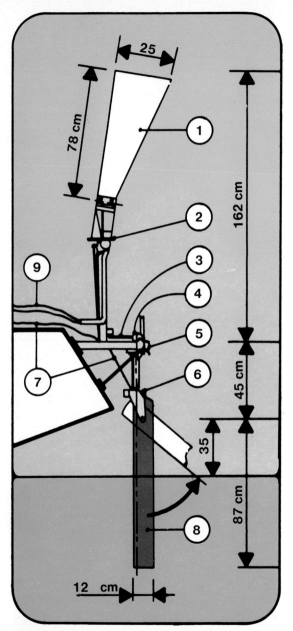

5.14. *The Atoms vane gear. 1, vane. 2, turret. 3, differential linkage between vane and pendulum. 4, tiller line sheaves. 5, supporting platform. 6, latch for pendulum. If a piece of wood is hit the latch allows the pendulum to lift without breaking. The pendulum can be returned to its position by pulling line 7. The manufacturer supplies and electric alarm which sounds when this latch is broken. 8, pendulum. 9, lines for course setting.*

over sheaves and down the centre of the "mast" on which the vane is fitted. At the bottom of the "mast" these wires pass over further sheaves to the quadrant on the stock of the steering part of the pendulum. When the fitting which supports the vane is turned to set the course the wires are twisted but, as the movement is restricted to 180° each way, this does not matter. The vane mounting is fitted with a grooved flange round which a wire is wound. By pulling one end or the other of this line the vane can be turned and set to fine limits, if needs be from the doghouse.'

The steering force delivered by the vane is so great that it is not always necessary to lead the tiller lines to the helm. In such cases the tiller lines (stays) are made fast on the "mast" and the pendulum acts like a normal auxiliary rudder. Now, as to performance:

The well-known ocean racer *Myth of Malham* was steered by a mini vane of 51×20 cm for 48 hours when running before a severe storm with the wind force varying between 8 and 9, and with high seas breaking over the cockpit from time to time. Skipper Noel Bevan said that mutual steering was impossible and, without the vane, he would have

5.15. *The differential linkage of the Atoms vane gear. Linkage is such that the initial deflection of the pendulum about its vertical axis is nullified as the pendulum swings to one side. If the pendulum swings out too far it corrects this itself. Because the vane has an inclined axis the force delivered is proportional to the degree of deviation from course and, consequently, the vane is able to deliver great steering power that is exactly proportional to the degree of deviation from course, without being dependent on an irregular balance of the forces that act on the pendulum and the rudder.*

had to heave to and ride out the storm. There are of course many sailors' yarns of this sort, but I have heard too many to dismiss them out of hand.

A weak point with this vane gear is that the pendulum is locked when the vane is not operating. If the tiller lines are merely freed the very heavy skeg cum pendulum can be broken by the violent movements of the stern, but if the skeg cum pendulum is fixed by the tiller lines there is a risk of breaking the frame on which the vane gear is mounted. Although the Gunning vane gear has a great history it is one of the earliest to have appeared and seems to have been superseded by more modern designs, particularly when weight and appearance are also taken into consideration.

Atoms (French)

The Atoms gear is deservedly the most popular French vane gear. The vane itself is small, elegant, develops great steering power and reacts quickly. Not for nothing do practically all French competitors in single-handed racing fit this gear. It has been successfully used in boats from 8 to 18 metres LOA, such as *Wild Rocket*, and works in just the same way as the Aries, for example. Spare

75

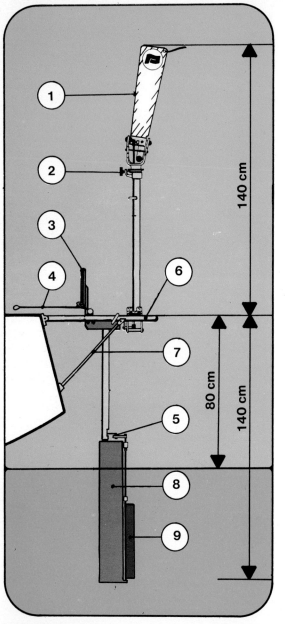

parts can easily be carried because the components are so small. The course is set with a worm, controlled by lines which are led to the cockpit. The manufacturer also supplies an electric motor to drive the worm, and the course can then be set by pressing a button. Very fine adjustment is possible. Differential linkage is used between the inclined axis vane and the pendulum. When the pendulum lifts to one side due to a certain deflection about its vertical axis this deflection is gradually reduced as the pendulum lifts further.

There is no need for inclined axis vanes to turn freely in the wind when the gear is not operating. The Atoms therefore cannot be un-coupled and this makes the course setting mech-anism simpler. To operate the gear the vane is aligned to the wind by the course setting line. It does not take up this position automatically as is the case with a free pivoting vane with vertical axis. The Atoms has a latch that holds the vane vertical when not being used.

5.16. *The Navik self-steering gear with inclined axis vane, paddle and trim tab. 1, vane. 2, knob for course setting. Unsuitable for remote control by line but electronic remote control is possible. 3, transmission quadrant. 4, tiller lines. 5, linkage with compensat-ing effect between the vane and the small trim tab. 6, tubular frame. 7, bracket. 8, paddle. 9, small trim tab.*

Navik (French)

The Navik self-steering gear uses a paddle actuated by a trim tab which is so small that only a small vane is needed to drive it. Although less robust than the Atoms wind vane, for example, the smaller size has definite advantages. Four Navik gears were used in the 1976 OSTAR and all were satisfactory. The gear can be used with a small electric motor that takes over the vane's duties, and the boat is then steered by a compass. The linkage between vane and trim tab has a compensating effect, and an inclined axis vane is used. There is no comparison when the paddle moves sideways. The gear operates similarly to gears such as the Atoms and the Aries, but its vane is the smallest to be used. All components are easy to replace and, like the vane gears already described, the paddle can easily be lifted out of the water and has a safety mounting, the paddle shaft being released if flotsam is hit before damage can occur.

With the Navik vane gear, just as with Atoms, a small electric motor can be used for course setting by remote control if the gear is too far away to reach the mechanical course setter. The course has to be set manually at the Navik's vane, and the mechanism cannot be worked by hand from a distance.

5.17. The Navik fitted to this boat is an elegant solution to the self-steering problem.

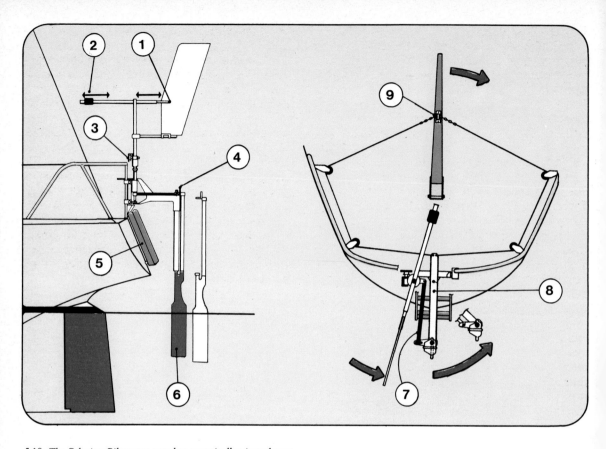

5.18. *The Schwing-Pilot vane gear has a vertically pivoted vane coupled to a vertical axis pendulum. 1, the vane can be moved along the shaft so that the force delivered by the vane matches the type of boat, and the counterweight 2 is therefore adjusted similarly. 3, knob to operate a worm which sets the course. 4, grip for removing the pendulum. 5, swimming ladder. 6, pendulum which pivots about two vertical axes instead of the normal combination of one vertical and one horizontal axis. 7, linkage between vane and pendulum. The initial angle of incidence of the pendulum that causes it to swing out is reduced as the pendulum swings out and steering consequently is proportional, just as with the Atoms pendulum vane. 8, pendulum control arm. 9, tiller lines made fast to the helm with a section of chain.*

Schwing-Pilot (German)

The Schwing-Pilot gear differs from other pendulum gears in that the pendulum turns about two vertical axes whereas a normal pendulum turns about one vertical and one horizontal axis. This simplifies the various linkage mechanisms, particularly because the vane is also vertically pivoted. When the pendulum is deflected by the vane it swings sideways round one vertical axis, and this reduces the risk of its coming out of the water as can happen with conventional pendulums. Steering is fully proportional and the linkage between vane and pendulum can be varied extremely simply. The vane can be moved along the strut to increase or decrease vane power. Course setting and the coupling of the vane to the linkage differ from the Hasler vertically pivoted vane gear. With its very careful construction this is a first class gear which can be expected to perform well, but it is really very expensive when compared to a conventional pendulum gear with inclined axis vane. The question is whether the improvement in performance matches the difference in price. The pendulum turns in the same direction as the rudder, and it can easily be used as an auxiliary rudder. An unusual point is the swimming ladder which is part of the frame.

Trim tab vane gears

Trim tab gears are very popular for home-construction, particularly when the boat has a rudder hung on the stern. Operation and construction are simple, and consequently trim tab vane gears are generally considerably cheaper than pendulum systems and others. The trim tab vane gears work reasonably well if differential linkage is used between vane and trim tab, and they can be fitted to boats with reasonable directional stability. The trim tab fitted to a conventional rudder is really unable to steady the boat when she yaws, and the lift force developed by the trim tab opposes the rudder's lift force, which means that the rudder's efficiency is decreased. A pendulum vane gear is preferable in these respects.

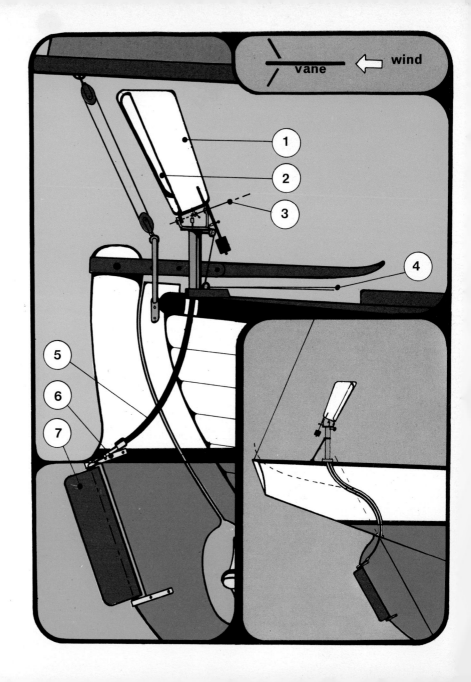

Crew (Norwegian)

The Crew vane gear is an original answer to the self-steering problem. The vane pivots about a steeply inclined axis and drives a trim tab through a flexible push-pull cable. The power and sensitivity of the vane are increased by two flaps attached to the trailing edge of the vane. Due to the few restrictions imposed by the flexible cable the vane can be sited anywhere on the boat. No differential linkage is used between vane and trim tab, but trim tab deflection is not affected by rudder movement. Friction in the flexible cable can cause problems, particularly after some time has elapsed. It appears too that a trim tab on a rudder with an inboard stock is not the most reliable solution to the self-steering problem.

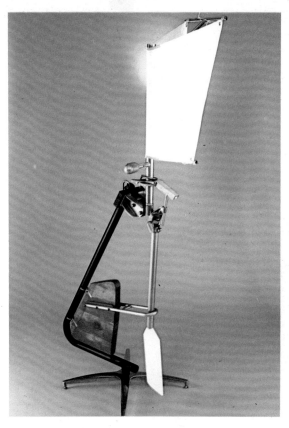

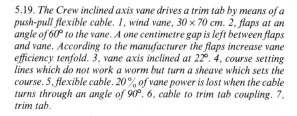

5.19. *The Crew inclined axis vane drives a trim tab by means of a push-pull flexible cable. 1, wind vane, 30 × 70 cm. 2, flaps at an angle of 60° to the vane. A one centimetre gap is left between flaps and vane. According to the manufacturer the flaps increase vane efficiency tenfold. 3, vane axis inclined at 22°. 4, course setting lines which do not work a worm but turn a sheave which sets the course. 5, flexible cable. 20 % of vane power is lost when the cable turns through an angle of 90°. 6, cable to trim tab coupling. 7, trim tab.*

5.20. *The Saye's Rig vane gear is an example of a vertical axis vane with a trim tab (pendulum) connected to the main rudder. Differential linkage is used between vane and trim tab.*

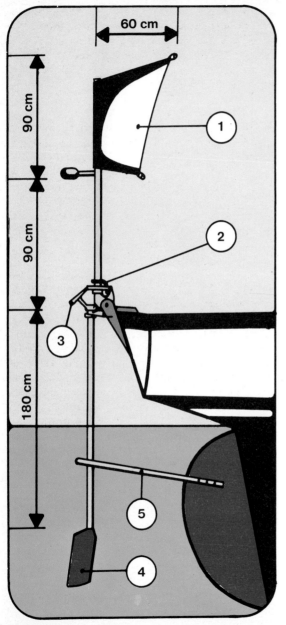

Saye's Rig (USA)

The Saye's Rig vane gear is a reliable trim tab system, suitable both for rudders with an inboard stock and for those hung on the stern. A wedge-shaped sail cloth vane drives a trim tab through differential linkage. The trim tab is suspended between the linkage mechanism and the 'tiller' which connects it to the rudder. The trim tab acts powerfully due to the considerable length of this tiller, and a small trim tab can therefore move large unbalanced rudders. The trim tab can also be removed easily, and this is unique where trim tabs act on rudders hung beneath the hull. When the rudder deflects the trim tab moves outwards too, just as a pendulum does, and this is why the manufacturer calls it a pendulum gear. This is not really true because this 'pendulum' serves the rudder blade as a trim tab would. The system does not counter yawing and, just like a normal trim tab, the rudder's steering force is reduced by the trim tab effect and not increased as it would be by a pendulum.

The cost matches that of a pendulum vane gear, but apart from the disadvantages just mentioned the Saye's Rig looks neat, dispenses with tiller lines and, last but not least, the trim tab moves to leeward when the boat's weather helm increases. There is consequently no danger of seeing it come out of the water to windward.

5.21. *The Saye's Rig vane gear. 1, wedge-shaped vane. 2, course setter. 3, differential linkage. 4, trim tab suspended like a pendulum. 5, the 'tiller' with which the trim tab actuates the rudder blade.*

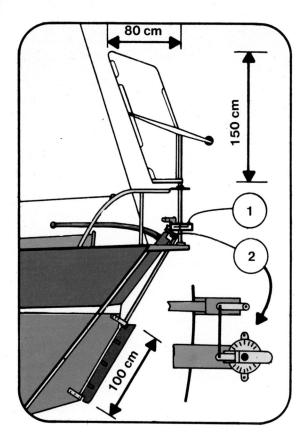

80 cm

150 cm

1

2

100 cm

5.22. *The Hasler vertically pivoted vane with servo-trim tab and stern hung rudder. This steering gear is assembled from components of the Hasler pendulum vane gear, but is naturally considerably cheaper. 1, vane coupling and course setter. 2, simple differential linkage.*

Hasler (UK)

Gibb markets an adaptation of the Hasler vane gear so that it can be used as a trim tab steering system. The vane is mounted on the boat herself, and is connected to the trim tab with differential linkage.

Quartermaster (UK)

The Quartermaster (figure 4.6) is a low price trim tab vane gear suitable for small boats with a rudder hung aft. The trim tab is suspended free of the rudder blade like the Saye's Rig gear. The vane is mounted on the rudder itself, and not on the boat. This ·naturally makes construction easier and reduces the cost, but makes it impossible to fit differential linkage.

Gears with direct rudder control

Vane gears that actuate the rudder directly are the simplest and cheapest gears available, but there are limits to their application. QME, Windpilot and Morris Marine (manufacturers of the Gunning wind vane) produce models of this type of vane. Being so simple they are very suitable for home construction as described in chapter 4.

The vane gears covered in this chapter are those that are best known. The great variety of different systems possible has by no means been exhausted, and it remains to be seen whether there can be real improvements in performance. It seems that it is improvement in the self-steering qualities of the boat and her rig that is being sought, rather than in vane gears. Using the apparent wind as the signal for setting the course continues to pose problems except when close hauled. Efficiency is improved remarkably by incorporating a second sensor, for example by using an overbalanced rudder. When it comes to adding a third sensor, however, namely boat speed, the cost becomes so exorbitant that it would be preferable to use an automatic pilot.

6 Automatic pilots for sailing boats

For and against vane gears

The number of self-steering gears fitted to sailing boats is increasing rapidly and they are not being used exclusively by cruising boats. Although modern vane steering gears are fully accepted there is still room for development and, latterly, the trend has been towards electronic self-steering using an automatic pilot.

Reliability is more important than efficiency or speed when under sail, and it is therefore easy to appreciate why the vane gears on the market are robust rather than elegant. It is to be hoped that the future will see a change in all the tubes, rods and lines that link the vane to the rudder. There are a few exceptions such as the Hydrovane which is a neat looking vane gear, while Atoms and others no longer offend the eye. However vane gears have the following disadvantages as well:

A They are vulnerable due to being mounted at the stern.

B Changes in the speed of both boat and wind cause the boat′ to go off course because the angle of the apparent wind is altered, and it is the apparent wind that determines the boat's course. A change in speed is an advantage when sailing close hauled but causes problems on all other courses. Vane gears can lose control of boats that are liable to accelerate extremely rapidly, such as catamarans.

C When controlled by vane gear the boat follows the wind. This is excellent for windward work, but when the sheets are freed the boat sails an oscillating course which diverges from the compass course desired. The boat may sail 10 to 20 miles further in 24 hours due to swinging either side of the course in response to the minor wind shifts that always occur. If the crew does not notice a permanent shift in the wind in good time (off-course alarm) a dangerous situation may arise.

D The wind vane is least effective, and may not work at all, on downwind courses when steering in any case is most problematical.

E The wind vane does not work when the boat is under engine.

In spite of these disadvantages a vane steering gear is nevertheless a useful self-steering aid, especially when the boat is on the wind. The advantages of wind vane gears are that they do not require electric current, that they can help to steady the boat and discourage yawing, that reaction to deviation from course is rapid, and that a great deal of power is provided to move the helm. These are the very points that can be the weaknesses of automatic pilots. In some circumstances, therefore, wind vane gears can perform better than automatic pilots, and vice versa.

My choice for a boat making a long ocean passage with a small crew would always be to fit a

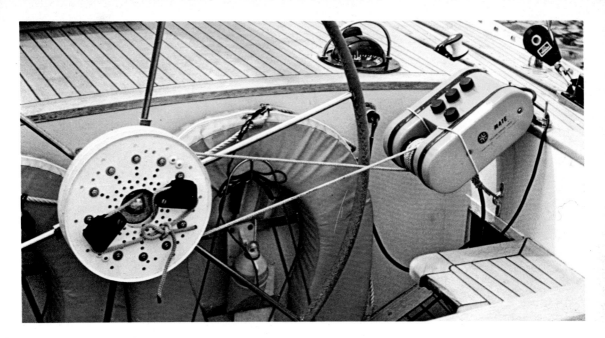

steering system that could be controlled by either a wind vane or an automatic pilot. As a last resort, should both give up the ghost, it would also have to be possible to trim the sails so that the boat could steer herself.

For and against automatic pilots

Automatic pilots have recently appeared on the market which meet the needs of sailing boats, and which do not suffer from the disadvantages listed from **A** to **E**. The technical development of small automatic pilots for sailing boats has resulted in systems that are both reliable and not too expensive. There is very little difference in price between automatic pilots for sailing boats and the better wind vane gears. These automatic pilots work just as well with a compass as with a wind vane, all components are below decks, and

6.1. *Here the Sharp Mate automatic pilot works the steering wheel of a modern ocean racer. This is a robust but simple automatic pilot with motor, controls and feedback incorporated as a single unit. Operation is adjusted with rudder, yaw and trim controls. A magnetic compass or a wind vane can be used for sensing, and the course is set at the sensor. The electric drive unit has an electro-magnetic clutch. In average weather conditions the power requirement is 2–3 amp hours with a 12 volt supply. Maximum pull on the tiller line is 45 kg (100 lbs), the line moves a maximum of 72 cm, and the automatic pilot takes 15 seconds to move the line this distance. Power unit output is one-twelfth hp. The steering compass in this photo will be useless because the automatic pilot's power unit is mounted too close to it.*

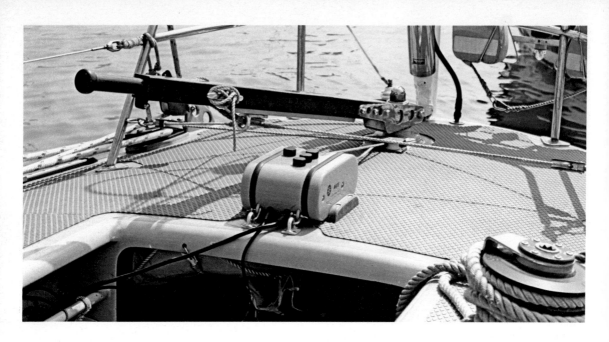

6.2. *The same automatic pilot as in figure 6.1 operates a tiller here. The Mate is fitted on board* BESTEVAER, *a single-handed racing yacht 16·40 metres in length. The Mate automatic pilot shown, with a power output of one-twelfth hp, was used in light weather but a more powerful unit was fitted when conditions were difficult. Both were well able to steer the boat, but the more powerful pilot's 'hard over' time was only 8 seconds. This was particularly important on down wind courses to avoid oversteering. When installing an automatic pilot care must be taken that it is not able to deflect the rudder so far that it comes up against the stops. Maximum deflection by the automatic pilot must occur earlier because otherwise the motor will be stopped and can be burnt out. The automatic pilot here has no protection from weather, water and wind, and it seems that few automatic pilots at present can survive this for long. A more protected position or better waterproofing is required.*

reliability is assured by the use of solid state circuits and linkages. They are efficient on all courses and are easy to adjust to the weather conditions.

The automatic pilot has a driving motor which moves the rudder. An electric motor is generally used, but hydraulic drive can be fitted for larger boats' rudders. The motor receives signals from a sensor which may be a compass or a wind vane, the latter being used for windward work and the compass for all other courses. The sensor's signal is amplified and passed via the control unit to the motor, while knobs on the control unit adjust the automatic pilot to the sailing conditions. The last and very important part of the automatic pilot is the 'feedback'. It is this that keeps the automatic pilot's reactions in proportion, correlating the amount of rudder applied to how far the boat is actually off course. Feedback ensures that the automatic pilot is not only aware of course deviation but also of the rudder's position so that it can match the rudder angle to the degree of deviation from course. The feedback is the sensor of the rudder's position.

Choice

Just as with wind vane steering gear, an automatic pilot must be chosen with care if optimum performance is to be obtained. The boat's inherent directional stability plays a part too, because a stable boat demands less of its automatic pilot than an unstable boat. Stability should not be thought of as a static condition. Behaviour with the helm lashed matters less than how the boat reacts to a correction after going off course. As already stated the result of deviation from course and subsequent course correction can be that the boat oscillates about the course desired. Some boats correct this automatically, others continue to oscillate to the same degree, while others deviate further each time they swing. Boats in the first category just need a simple automatic pilot with few controls, and cheaper models are therefore adequate. Boats in the second and third categories need a more sophisticated unit.

Oscillation either side of the course means oversteering, and this can be kept within permissible limits or even prevented entirely if the automatic pilot has suitable controls. It is only impossible to control boats that are particularly prone to yawing, because an automatic pilot has no inherent resistance to this and merely makes a correction following a deviation from course. More sophisticated pilots, such as those fitted to aeroplanes and large ships, incorporate an electronic control to counter yawing artificially, but up to now the automatic pilots designed for sailing boats rely on the boat herself to counter yawing.

Oscillating to a greater or lesser degree about the course cannot therefore always be arrested by

6.3. *A simple little magnetic compass can be used as the automatic pilot's sensor, the course being adjusted by turning the compass in relation to the boat's centreline. With a more sophisticated system the course is adjusted at the automatic pilot's control unit, and the compass can then be fitted at the most suitable place. This is a great advantage if the boat is made of steel.*

present-day automatic pilots but, given the right controls and fast enough rudder movement, the automatic pilot will in most cases be well able to keep the boat on course without oversteering becoming a major problem.

Naturally the steering power required is an important factor when choosing an automatic pilot, and this depends more on the type of rudder fitted to the boat than on her displacement and length.

According to the price automatic pilots offer more or less in the way of accessories, controls and so on. The rule that affects the choice is not 'the more expensive the better the automatic pilot' but 'the more expensive the greater the power consumption'. It is best to choose the simplest automatic pilot with the lowest power consumption that can steer the boat in the majority of circumstances, given a little help by trimming the sails correctly. Naturally there are power wasters that can keep the boat on course in all conditions with the sails completely unbalanced, but they use too much electricity and are expensive. A one-quarter or one-twelfth hp motor that can move the rudder from 15° to port to 15° to starboard in 10 seconds is adequate for most boats. The 21 metre ketch *Second Life* had a one-eighth hp motor, while the 14 metre sloop *Spirit of Delft*'s motor was one-twelfth hp. Both boats had efficient rudders requiring little steering power, and their directional stability was good. Only when off the wind in high seas did difficulties arise with *Spirit of Delft*'s automatic pilot because rudder movement was too slow to override oversteering. *Second Life* appears to have had better inherent directional stability because the automatic pilot served well even in difficult circumstances.

The single-handed racer *Bestevaer* had a very rapid rudder movement, 8 seconds to swing the rudder from 25° to port to 25° to starboard. This was due to fitting an electric motor with a very light armature, and a rudder (figure 2.8E) that

6.4. *A small electronic wind vane enables the automatic pilot to be steered in relation to the apparent wind when close hauled, but on other points of sailing a compass course is preferable. The course is adjusted by turning the wind vane in its holder. The vane is fitted to the windward guardrail. In more complicated systems a wind vane is mounted on top of the mast, and the course is then set remotely at the control unit.*

needed little power to move it. The automatic pilot was well able to meet the most difficult conditions with the spinnaker set.

A long 'hard over' time (small motor, low power requirement) is quite acceptable when sailing to windward but, if the automatic pilot is to be up to the situations that can arise, rapid and large rudder movement is required, and even this is not always enough to stop oversteering.

If a pendulum, trim tab or auxiliary rudder is used, just as for wind vane gears, only a small drive motor is needed. A pendulum or trim tab can be actuated by a very small electric motor, but great force will nevertheless be exerted on the rudder, and rudder movement will also be much faster. Given such a combination a normal vane gear can be used to actuate the same trim tab, auxiliary rudder or pendulum should the automatic pilot or the power supply fail.

This combination is particularly attractive for windward work because good wind vane gears can perform better on the wind than automatic pilots. The Navik self-steering gear is one that can also be fitted with a servo motor so that the boat can be steered by an automatic pilot.

Damping down yawing and rolling

A steering system with an auxiliary rudder controlled by an automatic pilot has its attractions too, not just because such a rudder requires little steering force but because the main rudder can be fixed and will contribute to the boat's stability.

Even better is a trim tab fitted to an over-balanced auxiliary rudder. This takes care of directional stability and the automatic pilot has but few course corrections to make. If a conventional rudder is fitted it is preferable for the automatic pilot to actuate a pendulum rather than a trim tab. At present the Sailomat vane gear (pendulum cum auxiliary rudder combination) is

6.5. *The Command Auto Pilot made by Space Age Electronics Ltd is an adaptable small automatic pilot suitable for wheel or tiller steering. The sensing device is either a wind vane, or the electronic polar locking unit shown here. This does the same job as a compass but reacts more quickly to deviations from course because it has no moving parts. Solid state motor controls are incorporated, and no electro-magnetic relays are used. The drive unit is of the variable speed type and is rated at one-tenth hp. The control unit is separate from the electric motor and has trim, yaw and rudder controls as well as red and green lights to indicate when the motor is working. This makes it easier to adjust the pilot to keep the battery drain to the minimum. The course is set at the sensor. Time is computed so that smaller alterations in course are disregarded, but larger and more persistent deviations from course result in immediate correction. Average power consumption is 3–6 amp hours with a 12 volt supply.*

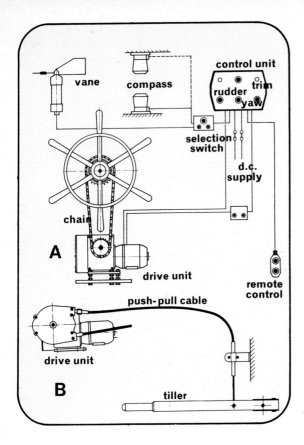

6.6. *A. Schematic diagram for the installation of the Command Auto Pilot with steering wheel. The feedback is integral with the drive unit.*
B. Schematic diagram for a tiller or rudder quadrant moved by a push-pull cable.

probably the most efficient self-steering gear available for sailing boats because the pendulum can be controlled either by the automatic pilot or by the wind vane.

An automatic pilot should perhaps incorporate a means of countering rolling when sailing downwind. Rolling is due to forces acting on the sails or to following seas, and can be reduced by countering with the helm at the right moment. An additional sensor in the form of an inclinometer is required if the automatic pilot is to be able to do the same. The performance of an automatic pilot downwind can be improved by adding any means of reducing rolling.

Position on the boat

When buying an automatic pilot it is important to bear in mind the positions where the components will be mounted. The motor etc must be a certain distance away from the compass, control knobs must be within easy reach and, if the boat is made of steel, considerable thought must be given to where to mount the compass. Most important of all is to be able to disconnect the automatic pilot immediately because the difference between life and death can be a question of seconds, for example when on a collision course. It must be possible to steer manually at any moment.

Controls

An automatic pilot has a number of controls to enable the way it steers the boat to be matched to the wind and sea conditions of the moment, and to avoid oversteering and wasting electricity. It is not only the automatic pilot that has to be adjusted; the sails must be trimmed properly to reduce the steering force required and to save the automatic pilot unnecessary work. The most usual controls are:

Rudder: This controls the amount of rudder applied. Although rudder deflection is automatically kept in proportion to course error the amount of rudder applied has to be adjusted to the weather and sea conditions. If the rudder deflects too far the boat will overswing, but if rudder movement is too small the boat is not returned to her course, or anyway not at the right time. Correct adjustment is very important.

Trim: This alters the nil position of the rudder from which corrective movements start. When sailing to windward the boat may be balanced when the rudder is deflected 5° to counter weather helm. The trim control sets the rudder at this angle of 5° and course corrections start from this nil position. If this is not done the rudder will return amidships after every correction, and in consequence the boat will immediately bear away from her course. By turning the trim control to, say 5° to leeward, unnecessary rudder movement and reduction in performance to windward are avoided. The trim control is used on other points of sailing as well.

Yaw: This control permits the boat to swing to a certain degree before the automatic pilot corrects the course. A correction is not needed every time the boat goes slightly off course because she will correct minor deviations herself. The automatic pilot only acts when the boat has gone further off course, beyond this dead band.

Time: This delays the automatic pilot's reaction. The sensor gives a signal but the automatic pilot waits for, perhaps, three seconds before making a correction. This delay can be adjusted to the state of the sea. The latest automatic pilots do not base course correction on the boat's heading after the three second delay but on the average course during those three seconds. The boat may have moved 5° off course at the end of three seconds but, if the average deviation during that time was 2°, the automatic pilot corrects for 2° and not for 5°.

Counter rudder: So far few automatic pilots incorporate this control which is superfluous for most sailing boats. It is used to discourage the boat from swinging, as has already been discussed. Counter rudder is applied by the automatic pilot in proportion to the rate at which the boat swings.

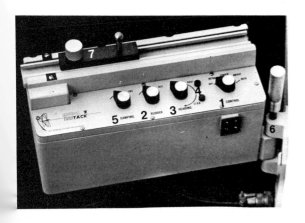

6.7. *The Iso Tack Auto Pilot is only suitable for tiller steering. The drive motor, control unit, feedback and course setter (compass) are incorporated as a single unit hung on the side of the cockpit with a hinged mounting (6). The tiller is fixed to a slide (7). The control unit has: 1, time control (damping). 2, rudder control. 3, course setter. 4, check lights to help with course setting and 5, on/off switch. Trim is adjusted mechanically by moving the slide manually. A wind vane mounted on top of the mast can be used as a sensing unit in place of the incorporated compass. The course is set as follows: put the boat on to the course desired, set knob (3) where both control lights (for port and starboard) light up, switch knob 5 and the automatic pilot takes over steering. Knob 3 can be turned to port or starboard to alter course and the boat responds immediately. Maximum force exerted on the tiller is 35 kg and the traveller can slide 25 cm. Power requirement averages 2–3 amp hours with a 12 volt supply.*

Thus the boat is brought back on course and counter rudder is applied in good time to prevent the boat swinging beyond her course.

By experimenting with these controls it is probably always possible to find a setting which not only keeps the boat on course but does so with the minimum of rudder movement and power consumption. As with vane gears it takes sensitivity to find the correct setting, as well as some knowledge of how the automatic pilot operates and of what it is capable. It is particularly worth while taking the trouble to find the exact settings for the different points of sailing when the automatic pilot has been fitted on board.

The control unit of some automatic pilots has a green and red light to help with adjustment. These shine when the motor moves the rudder to port or starboard and counting how often they light up every minute shows whether the automatic pilot has been set sufficiently accurately. These control lights are not needed if the control unit is close to the motor because you can then hear when and how often the motor works. Some of the more expensive models are set automatically, and if a unit has few control knobs it is either a very simple automatic pilot or one that adjusts itself automatically to the sailing conditions.

Course setting

Obviously the automatic pilot has to be set to the required course as well as to the weather and sea conditions. The course is related either to the direction of the wind or to a compass course. Wind direction is sensed by a small wind vane very similar to the wind direction indicators that have been used in boats for years. If a magnetic course is to be followed a compass is usually used as a sensor. The automatic pilot's steering compass is important: if it is not sufficiently sensitive performance is affected considerably and oversteering

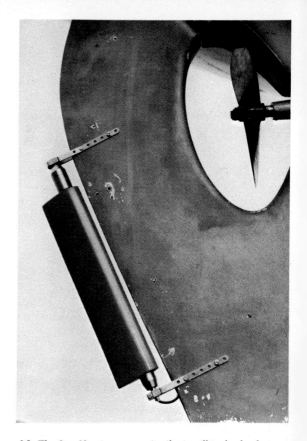

6.8. *The Oxy Nautica automatic pilot is still in the development stage but tackles the problem in an original way. The automatic pilot does not move the rudder directly but through a trim tab into which the drive motor is built. Battery drain is minimal with such a system, power consumption being 0·1 amps with a 12 volt supply. The trim tab can be deflected 30° either side and takes only 2 seconds to deflect this far, so the rudder movements required for course correction are made very quickly. The automatic pilot adjusts almost automatically to weather and sea conditions, and there is a 'counter rudder' control to prevent oversteering. Because the course is set at the control unit a wind vane at the top of the mast, or a conveniently sited compass can be used as sensors. A repeater can be provided for both wind vane and compass and can be used for normal navigation. The complete system is a good but expensive solution to self-steering problems.*

may result. Sensor and course setter are a single unit in most of the automatic pilots for sailing boats, the sensor itself being turned in relation to the boat's centreline to set the course. This is the simplest and cheapest system. The sensor then has to be fitted within easy reach, and preferably not too far from the control unit because sometimes both need to be adjusted simultaneously. The vanes of these automatic pilots cannot be mounted on top of the mast but are normally fitted on the guardrail (to windward). This is a satisfactory method because it is not a question of measuring the angle of the wind but of keeping a steady course in relation to the wind. Siting the compass in steel boats is not easy, and it may be advisable to have one compass for both the automatic pilot and for steering. If two compasses are used it is worth recommending that both should be compensated. It is essential to check that it is possible to site the sensor in a suitable place within easy reach before buying an automatic pilot.

The course is adjusted at the control unit of more sophisticated automatic pilots, and not at the sensor which can therefore be placed at any convenient position, with the wind vane probably at the top of the mast. Automatic course adjustment goes a step further. First the boat is put on course, then a knob on the control unit is pressed and held for a few seconds. The automatic pilot then takes control and keeps the boat on the course she was sailing during those few seconds. While the knob is depressed the sensor is turned by an electric motor to the course required. Although this method of course setting is easy enough to operate it is expensive and power consumption is high. A compromise is provided by Iso-Tack among others. The boat is first brought on course, and a knob on the control unit is then turned until a red and green light shine simultaneously. The automatic pilot is then ready to take control. The course can be adjusted very easily by turning the knob to port or starboard.

6.9. *Automatic pilots which can be fitted entirely below decks are much more reliable than those mounted in the cockpit. Attention must be paid to the linkage between steering motor and rudder shaft. Rack drive is used here, a short tiller driving the rudder stock by means of a rack. This is a neat method for boats with tiller steering. With wheel steering the drive motor is connected to the wheel axis by a chain and sprocket or to some other suitable point in the linkage between wheel and rudder stock. If hydraulic steering is used the automatic pilot can be incorporated into the hydraulic system very easily.*

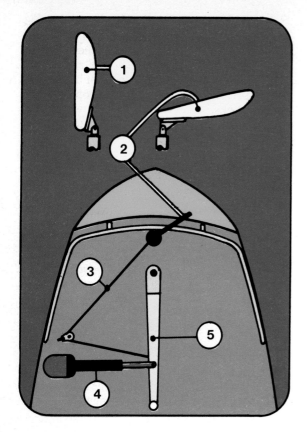

6.10. *The Autohelm combines a mechanical wind vane with an automatic pilot. Feedback, reduction of yawing, adjustment of trim and accurate correlation between applied rudder and off-course error are carried out mechanically, and the rudder is driven by a small electric servo-motor. The Autohelm is a cheap solution to the self-steering problem, for smaller boats. The actuator pushrod's stroke is 12·5 cm, maximum steering force is 41 kg and average power requirement is 3 watts (0·25 amps). The Autohelm Mk II incorporates a compass sensor. During the 1976 OSTAR the system did not appear reliable but the new version that has appeared since then has the following improvements:*

1 *When the vane is in this position it is very sensitive and responds to course deviations of 1°. The little wind vane, 20 cm long, is merely an electronic sensor and, unlike a wind vane that is part of a vane gear, delivers no force.*
2 *The vane is less sensitive in this position and, in heavy weather for example, will not make a correction until course error reaches 15°.*
3 *The feedback linkage is a cord connecting the tiller to the mast on which the vane is mounted. After deviating from course the vane electronically signals the motor which actuates the tiller. As the tiller moves the line is pulled and turns the wind vane transducer back to its original position where the electronic signal to the actuator stops.*
4 *Actuator unit.*
5 *Tiller.*

   Automatic pilots of this type, mounted as a single unit in the cockpit between the tiller and a fixed point, were very popular in the 1976 OSTAR and are available in many designs and sizes. Installation is simple and power consumption is small, but they suffer badly from vulnerability to sea water. Steering power is limited which restricts their use to smaller boats.

Off-course alarm and remote controls

Among the accessories available are an off-course alarm and remote control. The former sounds when the boat deviates from her course or when the wind direction changes. If the compass is acting as sensor the wind vane sounds the alarm, but when the wind vane is controlling the course the alarm is sounded by the compass. The alarm is so set that the boat is permitted to sail for a certain time off course, and also to go some way off course. Otherwise there would be little peace on board because it is rare for a boat to be dead on course. The off-course alarm enables a more or less optimum course to be sailed without having to watch the automatic pilot constantly.

Remote control consists of a knob or button which is connected by cable to the automatic pilot's control unit, and it can be used to steer the boat from the cabin in bad weather. When sailing single-handed remote control makes it possible to work on the foredeck, for example, and to alter the boat's course simultaneously to suit. Remote control is also useful for small temporary adjustments to course, such as when giving way to a boat on the opposite tack. After switching off the remote control the boat reverts to her previous course with the setting unchanged. If the setting is changed when altering course, bringing the boat back to her original course obviously means resetting the automatic pilot.

Linkage

The last part to be considered is the linkage between the motor and the boat's steering mechanism. There are many possible systems but problems can be avoided by giving the matter some thought before buying an automatic pilot. If the boat has a tiller this may be moved back and forth on a slide by the automatic pilot, or may be connected to a reel on the motor by lines. A wheel is more complicated. It can also be moved by line, but this will only work well if the linkage between wheel and rudder is very direct. If not, chain and sprocket linkage is preferable. Push-pull cables and shafts that act directly on the rudder quadrant are also used.

The motor in the systems shown here generally has a mechanical clutch engaged remotely by push-pull cable or directly by a lever on the motor itself. More expensive automatic pilots have an electro-magnetic clutch which makes installation and control easier, but always involves greater power consumption. Whatever linkage is used it must be strong.

Electro-hydraulic automatic pilots

An electro-hydraulic automatic pilot is more expensive and more complicated than an electronic automatic pilot, but is certainly worth considering for larger boats. The force needed to move the rudder is supplied by oil pressure, so electricity is used only for the electronic controls and power consumption is therefore very low. An oil pump driven by the propeller shaft supplies the oil pressure. In single-handed races an alternator has also to be driven by the propeller shaft to generate the power required because regulations specify that the boat's circuit must not be used for this purpose. It is then simpler if the propeller shaft drives a more powerful alternator which can generate adequate current for a completely electric automatic pilot.

The oil pump is the weak link in the chain of an electro-hydraulic automatic pilot. The rotational speed range of the pump is small and, in consequence, the boat speed at which the automatic pilot should work at its best has to be calculated beforehand. A variomatic type linkage between propeller shaft and oil pump can be the solution. Automatic pilots of this type are unnecessarily complicated and expensive, even for yachts like *Second Life*, and are really worth considering only when a boat has a hydraulic steering system anyway.

There are also hydraulic automatic pilots which work entirely independently of electricity, but those available are really far too complicated and expensive to be of interest to a yacht owner, unless race regulations exclude the use of electronic automatic pilots for single-handed racing.

Oversteering

Oversteering can be a problem when automatic pilots are operating, and the uncomfortable feeling of a boat oscillating continuously about her course to a greater or lesser extent certainly does nothing to add to the pleasures of sailing, quite apart from there being a danger of a breakaway when she will not return to her course. It is therefore undoubtedly worth taking the trouble to trace the cause of oversteering and to remedy it. Oversteering can be due to:

A Friction This causes the steering system to

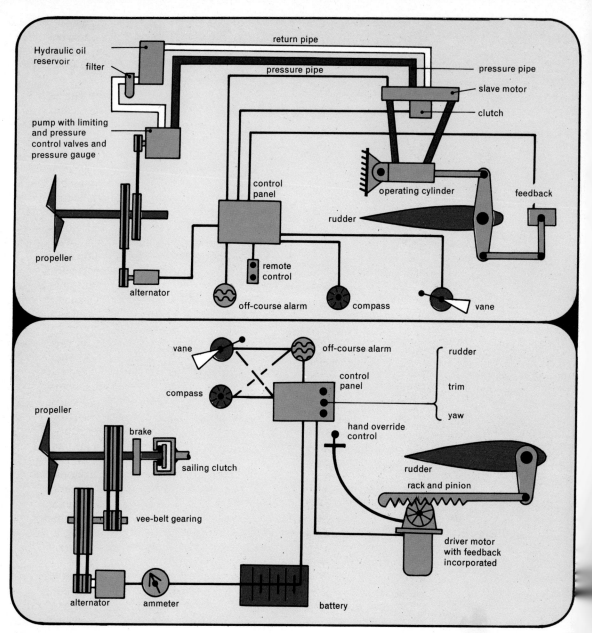

6.11. *Schematic diagram for an electro-hydraulic automatic pilot with the propeller shaft driving both an oil pump and an alternator. The latter only has to provide power for the electronic parts and can therefore be small. The oil pump is responsible for steering power. The hydraulic power unit that actuates the piston is controlled by the automatic pilot. The position of the rudder is monitored by a separate sensor and feedback ensures that rudder deflection matches off-course error. It is only sensible to use a hydraulic automatic pilot when the boat has hydraulic steering. Otherwise it is cheaper and easier to fit an electric automatic pilot.*

6.12. *Schematic diagram for an electro-mechanical automatic pilot such as used by* SECOND LIFE *for the 1972 OSTAR. The various details are self-evident. An alternator connected to the propeller shaft provides the current. When the boat's course is sensed by the compass the alarm is sounded by the apparent wind sensor, and vice versa.*

work too slowly. Course corrections will be too late, the boat too far off course before she starts to respond and, when she does, the effect is so great that she shoots through her proper course.

B *Play* Play in the linkage has the same effect as excessive friction and must be reduced to a minimum if the automatic pilot is to operate well.

C *Inertia* The mass of the moving parts of both automatic pilot and steering gear causes a definite delay in reaction to going off course. Generally speaking it is desirable to keep the weight of the moving parts as low as possible.

D *Speed of rudder movement* This is normally the main culprit. The rudder must react sufficiently quickly to a deviation from course because, otherwise, course correction trails behind course error and the automatic pilot cannot control the boat. The same occurs if the drive motor is not powerful enough to deflect the rudder satisfactorily.

First try to remedy this by varying the drive ratio between motor and rudder. Although the motor's output is fixed the way in which power is used can be varied. For example rudder can be applied quickly with low steering force, or more slowly with greater force. If varying the ratio fails to produce satisfactory results an automatic pilot with a more powerful motor is required, or, alternatively, the rudder should be replaced by one that requires less steering force. Should oversteering occur only in exceptional sailing conditions weigh this up against the fact that, for the rest of the time, a smaller automatic pilot with lower power requirement is preferable.

E *Time lag* This is the interval between the moment when the boat goes off course and the moment when the motor starts to correct her. It is the quality of the sensor and the

electronic circuitry that decide the delay. In some circumstances very quick reactions are required, and the automatic pilot must be capable of this, but the time lag should be adjustable so that reaction can be slowed as desired to suit the conditions.

If oversteering cannot be prevented by the measures described above the boat has only moderate directional stability, does not herself resist yawing, and needs an automatic pilot with a 'counter rudder' control. This refinement is not necessary for the majority of boats and current automatic pilots generally perform satisfactorily.

6.13. Smaller automatic pilots, and particularly those made as a single unit, cost much the same as better wind vane steering gears. More sophisticated automatic pilots installed below deck are in the same price range as expensive wind vane gears such as the Mustafà and the Sailomat. Everything has its price and, obviously a more expensive automatic pilot such as the Neco shown here can be expected to operate more reliably than cheaper models.

A compass and a wind vane sited on top of the mast are used as sensors. The course is set at the control unit which also has the normal rudder, trim and yaw (sensitivity) controls. The standard electric drive unit is a one-eighth hp motor which moves the rudder through full range in 15 seconds and drives a component of the steering gear by a chain and sprocket. The motor drives the output shaft through an electro-mechanical clutch, and limit switches are fitted to prevent mechanical damage. If the current drops the steering motor cuts out automatically so that steering can be taken over manually. A mechanical clutch is preferable for sailing boats, not only because battery drain is lower but because the clutch can be used to fix the rudder when the automatic pilot is not being used.

Weak points

Automatic pilots have a number of weak points, a few of which will be mentioned here. By no means all automatic pilots are unreliable in these respects, but these are points to watch out for. Corrosion is a permanent problem, especially when automatic pilots are mounted entirely or partly in the open. During the 1976 OSTAR many of the small automatic pilots suffered from corrosion and stopped operating. All components must be very carefully waterproofed, or a more protected position found. Anti-corrosive blocks, such as Storsafe, can be used to protect the inside of the automatic pilot. They give off a vapour that settles as a film of grease which effectively protects against corrosion all the components with which it comes into contact.

Connectors are used when removable automatic pilots are fitted in the cockpit, and are a constant source of trouble unless they are regu-

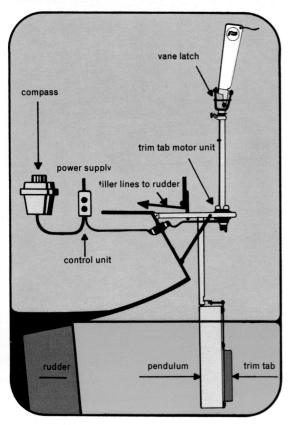

compass

vane latch

trim tab motor unit

power supply

tiller lines to rudder

control unit

rudder

pendulum

trim tab

6.14. *The Navik wind vane (Plastimo) can be obtained with a small electric motor that actuates the trim tab on the pendulum, thus combining the advantages of wind vane gears with those of automatic pilots. The steering motor uses the minimum of power and the provision of this can scarcely cause problems. The vane is used as course sensor for windward work, but the compass is used for all other points of sailing. On downwind courses the benefits of pendulum systems remain, such as countering yawing, developing great steering power and rapid rudder deflection.*

larly sprayed or smeared with an anti-corrosive such as acid-free vaseline. Only best quality aeroplane plugs and sockets should be used.

The relay can also cause problems. Several spares should be carried and it is advisable to check the contacts regularly for signs of burning. Careful adjustment of the automatic pilot to limit the number of operations per minute will lengthen the life of the relay considerably. Automatic pilots with motors of one-tenth hp or less use solid state circuitry in place of an electro-magnetic relay.

Blown fuses result from overloading the motor. They are of course fitted for this purpose and it can hardly be considered an unnecessary luxury to have enough spares on board.

The clutch between the motor and the steering system is subject to heavy loads and requires particular attention. Some manufacturers wrongly base their calculations on the power output of the motor rather than on the force that can be exerted by the rudder in difficult circumstances. Most clutches have a slip facility to prevent clutch damage or burning out the motor. Both this slip facility and the clutch itself may be weak points.

Failure of this sort is of course more likely when the automatic pilot is clearly inadequate for the boat to which it is fitted. This is one consequence of the need to keep power consumption low.

By no means is everything as rosy as it would appear. As already stated at the beginning of this chapter automatic pilots have their disadvantages. There is more to using an automatic pilot than just turning a knob to get the boat to continue on her course.

7 Providing electric current

Systems

The Single-handed Trans-Atlantic Race regulations prohibit the use of generators driven by combustion engines to provide the electric current for an automatic pilot. This led to the rapid development of apparatus that could generate current purely from 'natural' resources, and wind generators, water generators and solar cells were used in the 1976 OSTAR.

Obviously every long distance sailor is attracted to the idea of generating current without using the engine. Solar cells and wind generators also work when the boat is not making way and, consequently, are of interest to anyone who prefers to be independent of the shore. Even the low output of small systems can keep the battery charged to the right level and prevent self-discharge so that, even after some weeks absence, the skipper finds the battery's voltage level is sufficient to start the engine immediately. Water generators normally only charge when the boat is moving, and a system can therefore be assembled that supplies the total power requirement from natural resources. Ideally such a system should be comprised of two types of generators that compensate for each other's disadvantages. It should be borne in mind that these systems are better suited to continuous low charging rather than brief periods of high charging.

Water generator

A water generator is the most attractive way for a moving boat to obtain a reasonable supply of electric current, but this is provided at the cost of increased resistance. Although boat speed suffers the reduction in speed should not be excessive and will generally be between 1% and 5%.

Water generators either consist of an alternator connected to the propeller shaft (see figure 6.11) or an apparatus hung outboard on the transom.

When the propeller shaft drives an alternator the smallest propellers to produce useful output are, for example, a 19" × 10" two-bladed propeller for a yacht 36 feet LWL, or a 15" × 9" three-bladed propeller for a yacht 30 feet LWL. Smaller boats generally move too slowly and have too small propellers for this system to be used successfully. Propellers with a blade to area ratio of at least 35% are preferable. Propeller shaft friction should be minimal and, with this in mind, it is better to have a shaft that rotates in an oil bath bearing. A sailing clutch is required to isolate the propeller shaft from the engine, as well as a brake so that repairs can be made while the boat is under way. The shaft also has to be stopped to engage the sailing clutch, otherwise the boat has to be brought to a halt and this means a lot of work for the single-handed sailor.

A sailing clutch is essential if the boat has

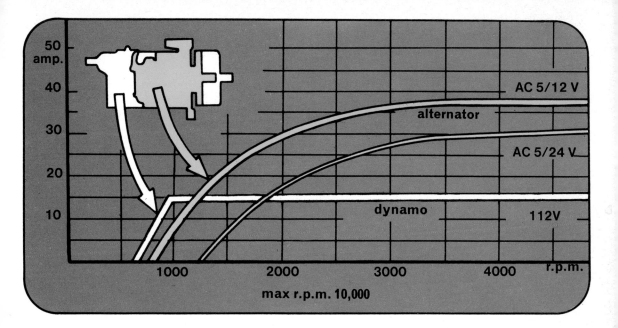

50 amp.
40 — AC 5/12 V
30 alternator
20 AC 5/24 V
10 dynamo 112V
1000 2000 3000 4000 r.p.m.

max r.p.m. 10,000

hydraulic reverse and reduction gear because a gear that continues to rotate when the engine is not running will be damaged by lack of lubrication. Although mechanical clutches do not have this trouble, and no sailing clutch is required when they run freely, friction is reduced and the cut-in speed of the charging systems drops by one knot if the propeller shaft can be isolated from the generator.

The moment required to start the propeller turning is fairly high, and always higher than that required to keep the shaft turning once it has started rotating. The shaft sometimes has to be turned by hand to encourage it to get going, or the course can be altered if this increases boat speed slightly. When the voltage level of the battery is low the alternator tries to charge it as quickly as possible, and the moment required to drive the alternator is then so great that the system cannot operate when the boat is moving slowly. Lowering

7.1. *The CAV marine alternator's charging curve. The 12 volt model cuts in at 800 rpm whereas the 24 volt model's cut-in speed is some 1200 rpm. Maximum permissible speed is 10,000 rpm. Alternators are used for water generators, practically without exception and a dynamo's charging characteristics are also shown for comparison. The dynamo is much larger and heavier and output is considerably lower. It is important that only alternators designed for marine service are used. They are fitted fairly low, not far from the propeller shaft, and even a small amount of water in the boat will be splashed about by the turning shaft and the drive belt. An alternator that has not been properly protected from water will have a very short life in a boat.*

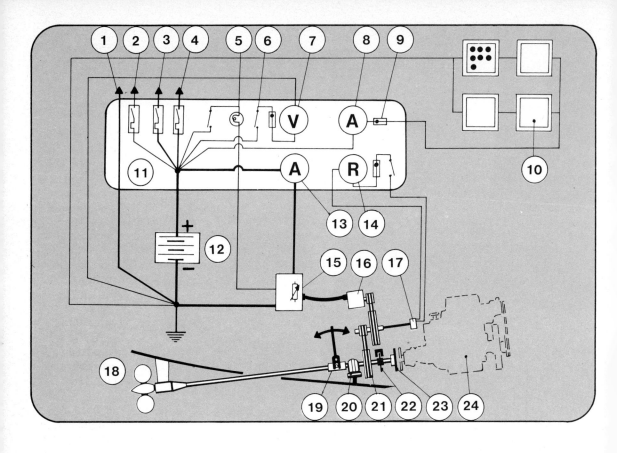

the field voltage with the help of a rheostat reduces the moment, and alternator output can then be matched to boat speed. A step-up pulley drive is fitted between the propeller shaft and the alternator to increase the rotation rate to a speed suitable for the alternator. The normal pulley ratio is from about 1:4 to 1:6, and is determined by the maximum propeller shaft rpm under engine. The alternator's maximum permissible speed of 10,000 rpm must not be exceeded when the engine is running. A pulley ratio of 1:5 between shaft and alternator can safely be used with an engine that

7.2. The system used on board BESTEVAER *for the 1976 OSTAR combined solar cells with a water generator.*

1   *Automatic pilot earth.*
2   *Power feed for electronic part of the automatic pilot, protected by a fuse.*
3   *Power feed for the light weather automatic pilot's drive motor.*
4   *Power feed for the heavy weather automatic pilot's drive motor. It is important that the power feed for the electronic part of the automatic pilot is kept separate from that for the drive motor to avoid voltage drop when the drive motor is operating. A drop in voltage is not so serious for the drive motor but can prevent the electronic parts working properly.*
5   *Warning lamp. This does not shine when the alternator is charging but lights up when it is working too slowly to charge the battery if the alternator switch is on. When not in use the battery isolating switch is left off to break the circuit and prevent battery discharge.*
6   *Switch which breaks the circuit to the voltmeter to prevent battery discharge.*
7   *Voltmeter, indicates the battery's voltage level.*
8   *Ammeter, 0–2 amps, to measure the charge delivered by the solar cells.*
9   *Glass fuse.*
10 *Solar cell panels. The maximum output of all four panels is 1·2 amps/24 volts.*
11 *Instrument panel.*
12 *Batteries, 60 amp-hours, 24-volts.*
13 *Ammeter, 0–40 amps, with enlarged cut-in scale, to measure the charge delivered by the alternator.*
14 and 17. *Propeller shaft tachometer, 0–1500 rpm.*
15 and 16. *CAV AC 5/24 alternator and regulator. The field voltage regulator is incorporated in the regulator housing. Alternator regulator and connecting cables are fully screened to prevent radio interference.*
18 *Verhey variable pitch propeller, diameter 40 cm.*
19 *Blade pitch control lever.*
20 *Thrust bearing.*
21 *Step-up pulley drive, ratio 1:5.*
22 *Propeller shaft brake.*
23 *Sailing clutch. This sailing clutch can be very simple because the propeller shaft is supported by the thrust bearing and can therefore be completely isolated from the gearbox.*
24 *Volvo MD2B diesel engine.*

The water generator cuts in at three knots if the sailing clutch has been disengaged. When battery voltage level is low and the boat is sailing at seven knots the generator charges at 10 amps/24 volts. Propeller blade pitch should be increased greatly at speeds over eight knots to prevent the propeller shaft rotating too fast.

does not run very fast and with a normal gear ratio. The alternator will then start charging at a satisfactory sailing speed of about three knots. Naturally a high pitch propeller and/or a propeller shaft that does not run freely will raise the minimum speed at which the alternator starts charging.

If the boat is fast and surfs easily the propeller may rotate too quickly and the alternator's safe operating speed could be exceeded. The remedy is to use a lower pulley ratio so that propeller speed cannot push the alternator over the limit, but inevitably the boat will then have to be sailing rather faster at cut-in speed, the lowest speed at which the system can operate. In extreme circumstances such as surfing a brake can be used to stop the shaft, but the best solution is to fit a variable pitch propellor, and to increase the pitch when the boat is moving fast so as to keep rotational speed under control. A fast-moving propeller is very noisy and by varying the pitch both rotational speed and noise can be kept down. At the same time the load on the stuffing box is reduced and leaks are less likely to occur. A variable pitch propeller can be feathered when not in use so as to reduce resistance.

The alternator is connected in the normal way to the battery, and both a warning light and an ammeter must be incorporated in the circuit in some conspicuous place where they can easily be seen. The whole installation should be so laid out as to avoid radio interference.

Propeller shaft installations were the only water generators used in 1972, but it is clear from the above that this is a complicated system with many snags. The first use of water generators hung outboard on the transom or towed astern like a log was in 1976.

A portable water generator has many advantages: no propeller shaft leaks, no propeller noise, cheap, no installation costs, minimum resistance in the linkage between propeller and alternator,

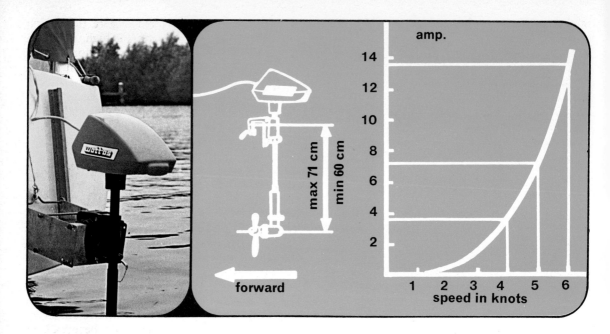

7.3. *The Watt-As water generator is hung on the stern like an outboard engine. A propeller can also be fitted permanently beneath the hull but this seems less interesting to me because when not in use or when damaged, say with a rope fouling the propeller, the water generator cannot be hauled on deck. As the Watt-As was designed specifically for generating power it is hardly surprising that it performs considerably better than a propeller shaft installation with a propeller of the same diameter. The loading curve shows this clearly. The three-bladed propeller has a diameter of 35 cm and the pitch is very low so a transmission ratio of 1:2 between propeller and alternator enables the alternator to cut in at a speed as low as two knots. Propeller speed is 1200 rpm at 6 knots. Again an alternator is used, while a regulator governs the output and a warning lamp lights when the generator is not charging.*

An alternator will damage its diodes irreparably if it turns without being connected to the battery, and the Watt-As incorporates diode protection. This is also the reason why there is no main switch in the layout in figure 7.2, so making it impossible to break the circuit between alternator and battery accidentally. Given similar output this type of water generator obviously offers less resistance than a propeller shaft installation.

The propeller points forwards and therefore works in undisturbed waterflow. Because it acts as a turbine the blades are curved in the opposite way to a normal boat propeller's blades.

The output of the Watt-As is 0·25 amps at 1·5 knots, and 9·5 amps at 5·5 knots with a 12 volt system. The drop in speed of a 12 metre boat amounts to about 3%. Maximum output occurs at seven knots and the generator must not be used at higher speeds.

minimum water resistance, and a propeller designed for the purpose. These generators cut in at very low boat speeds and, for a given output, resistance is lower than that of propeller shaft installations. Furthermore thay can be taken right out of the water when not in use, or to make repairs.

At a boat speed of six knots the water generator's output can reach 10 amps at 12 volts.

Wind generators

Wind generators are often used to generate electricity on land, especially in remote places and where power requirement is low. Originally thoughts on boat generators turned in this direction, but windmill-driven alternators are not really so satisfactory for boats under way. There has to be a large installation aft and, due to the lower apparent wind speed when sailing downwind, they are then less effective, their output being lowest just when it ought to be at its maximum. If output is to be adequate the generator has to be large and expensive. A much larger propeller than that of a water generator has to be used to generate the same amount of current because the density of air is 810 times lower than that of water. Wind speed is often considerably higher than water speed and, in a storm, there is a risk that the windmill will turn so fast that centrifugal force literally breaks it up. The windmill blades therefore have to be as light as possible and, for safety, the blade pitch of larger models alters as soon as rotational speed becomes excessive. Windmills cannot be said to improve the appearance of the boat, especially as they have to be installed where they cannot endanger the crew. Several of the 1976 OSTAR boats had small windmills which provided adequate current for the smallest automatic pilots, or contributed to the total current requirement. Some of these generators were sited above the mizzen where they could benefit from the stronger wind up high. When the boat is lying at anchor wind generators are an attractive power source, particularly in areas where there is little sun and much wind, but although solar cells are expensive they are indicated where there is much sun and little wind. Windmills may turn about a horizontal axis and they require a vane to turn them into the wind. Some have a vertical axis and the wind direction becomes unimportant. Construction is simpler, less room is required and installation is easier because there is no need to allow for the full turning circle of a conventional windmill.

An output of 2 amps/12 volts in a 20 knot wind can be expected from a wind generator that is not excessively large, but output such as the 10 amps produced by a water generator when the boat is making six knots is beyond the generator's capacity and would inevitably involve an impossibly large windmill. The resistance offered to air flow by the wind generator is beneficial on downwind courses but, when sailing to windward, this extra resistance has a considerable adverse effect.

Solar cells

A small contribution to the power supply can also be made by solar cells, which are photoelectric cells that convert the sun's energy directly into electricity. They work on the same principle as the photo-electric cells in a light meter, for example. This source of power does not affect the boat's performance under sail in any way, the only disadvantage being the high price which is due to the expensive material of which the cells are made, silicon. One strip of five cells generates about 2.3 volts, so the maximum output of a standard panel of 30 cells is 0·6 amps/12 volts. Output depends on light intensity and the position of the panel in relation to the sun. During the summer 25 amp

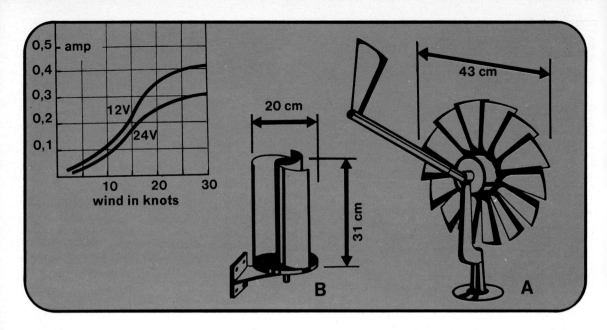

7.4. *A. The Aerocharge 3 is one of the smallest wind generators, with an output comparable to that of one panel of solar cells. In northern Europe the output of a wind generator such as this is 50 amp hours per week (12 volts) in average summer weather conditions. The graph shows how wattage varies with wind speed, and it is striking that the output of the same windmill diameter of 43 cm is greater with a 24 volt system than with a 12 volt system. A windmill with a diameter of 67 cm generates 0·3 amps (12 volts) with a 10 knot wind, and 2 amps with a 20 knot wind, while a windmill with a diameter of 100 cm generates 1·2 amps at 10 knots.*
B. Windmills that turn about a horizontal axis have to use a wind vane to keep them facing into the wind, and this involves more complicated construction as well as requiring a lot of room to allow it to turn full circle. The Eodyn wind generator solves this problem by rotating about a vertical axis, regardless of wind direction. This type of wind generator performs well and generates three-quarters of the Aerocharge's output in spite of its smaller size.

7.5. *These are two of the four solar cell panels fitted to* BESTEVAER. *The cells are encapsulated in a transparent block that is resistant to all weather conditions and is so strong that it can be trodden on. Solar cells were very popular with the 1976 OSTAR competitors. Maximum output of one panel is 0·6 amps at 12 volts.*

hours can be expected per week in the latitude of northern Europe, and this is of interest to the weekend sailor because the current consumed during the weekend will be replaced during the week. Obviously more than one panel is required if this source of power is to be used for longer periods. At least two, and preferably four panels are needed to generate power for a small automatic pilot during the summer. Many square metres of solar cells would be required for the boat's general requirements, and the price is prohibitive, quite apart from practical difficulties. It is not easy to find space for the panels although the ones now available are strong enough to be trodden on. The strips of cells have been replaced by a rectangular block made of transparent elastic material in which all thirty cells are encapsulated. These blocks can easily be fitted at deck level and will not crack as a result of boat movement etc, nor can they be damaged if, say, a winch handle is dropped onto them.

7.6. For the 1972 OSTAR STRONGBOW *had a small wind generator which powered a light automatic pilot. The generator's position on the afterdeck seems too vulnerable, and it was in fact swept overboard in the first storm. A reserve wind vane (QME) is stowed on the afterdeck.*

8 Using the sails to steer the boat

was to get the sails to steer the boat. Special sails that act more or less like a large wind vane can be used, such as 'Miranda' in figure 8.1, or just the sails that are a normal part of the boat's gear. Sails used for steering are generally connected directly to the tiller, but this is by no means always the case and they can sometimes be set so that the boat keeps herself on course. Twin headsails set in a vee forward are a good example of this.

Steering with sails

Little gear is needed to get the sails to steer the boat, two blocks, two small lines and some elastic strops are usually sufficient. Given a little experience it takes little time to trim and adjust the sails, once the right setting has been found. It is much easier if the fact that sails will be used for steering has been taken into account when deciding where to place the fittings on deck. A number of methods are shown in the following pages and from these a system suitable for every boat can be assembled. They are grouped according to the boat's course in relation to the apparent wind, specific systems being given for sailing close hauled, with a beam wind and down wind.

The genoa, staysail, mizzen, mainsail and spinnaker can all be used for steering. There are two ways of using the staysail. When it is set normally to leeward it both drives the boat forward and steers her. When it is backed it can be used when the wind is blowing from a wider range of directions, but it does not then contribute to boat speed.

Self-steering

A boat can sometimes keep herself on course without help purely due to her inherent directional stability. Trimming the sails and giving the rudder the right degree of bias is all that is needed to keep her steady. There are few problems when close hauled but not many boats are so stable on all the other points of sailing. Nowadays, with such good self-steering systems on the market, it is unnecessary to aim for such extreme directional stability when designing a boat because it is only obtained at the cost of other design requirements such as behaviour or performance under sail and manoeuvrability.

Furthermore the balance of a boat under sail is governed by the strength of the wind and the state of the sea. When the wind changes the sails have to be retrimmed if the boat is to stay on the desired course.

Wind vane steering gears and automatic pilots are a good solution to the self-steering problem, of course, but they are expensive and can fail. An alternative method used in years gone by

How they work

It is difficult to explain how sails steer a boat but it is easier to visualise when the wind is free or abeam. The sail must react both when the boat

109

8.1. *'Miranda' is what Sir Francis Chichester called the wind vane that he used in 1960 during the first Single-handed Trans-Atlantic Race. It was a small rotating mizzen which steered the boat with tiller lines. The little sail could be reefed in heavy weather and is really more properly classified as a sail used for steering rather than a wind vane gear. If classed as a sail used for steering it is over-complicated and one of the suggestions in this chapter is preferable, but if classed as a wind vane it has already long been superseded by modern and more efficient systems.*

goes off course and when wind strength alters. There must be a definite change in the tension of the sheet (tiller line) when the boat bears away or luffs up and this alteration in tension moves the rudder in such a way as to bring the boat back to her original course. A change in wind strength also alters the tension on the sheet, and when it blows harder the greater tension pulls the tiller to windward, thus countering the extra pressure exerted on the rudder as a result of the increase in weather helm. Clearly the sail has a double task when steering.

On one side the tiller is controlled by a rubber strop and rudder pressure, and on the other side by the sheet (tiller line) of the sail that is steering. The sheet has to be attached to windward of the tiller if the sail is to be able to perform both tasks.

As an example, the way a genoa steers on a reach (see figure 8.7A) is as follows:

1   As the boat bears away the tension on the sheet eases because the sail stalls. The angle of incidence is too great and the air stream to leeward becomes turbulent all over the lee side of the sail. The mainsail simultaneously blankets more of the genoa. The rubber strop pulls the tiller to leeward and the boat returns to her course.

2   As the boat luffs up the angle of incidence improves while the mainsail blankets less of the genoa, and the result is that the increased tension on the sheet brings the boat back on course, countering rudder pressure and the resistance of the rubber strop.

The forces on the rudder, the rubber strop and the sheet act together to keep the boat on course and, in these examples, the sail's efficiency is also affected by the apparent wind which increases when the boat luffs up but decreases when she bears away. This adds to the effects of the variations in sheet tension.

The increase in weather helm resulting from the stronger wind can be balanced because the

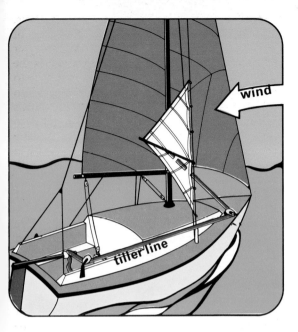

8.2. *A storm jib can be used to steer the boat and is hanked to the windward shroud when the wind is abeam but to the backstay on a run. The system is shown here at its simplest. The turning moment delivered by the sail equals the turning moment that the tiller must deliver to counter weather helm. Only one tiller line is being used, and the balance is found by making the tiller line fast further forward or further aft on the tiller, or by adjusting the spar that extends the clew of the storm jib. The angle of the jib to the wind can also be altered so that the force delivered matches the steering force required at the tiller. The jib sets better when the boat luffs up and pulls on the tiller line, returning the boat to her course. If the wind blows harder weather helm increases, pressure on the jib also increases and the tiller is pulled to windward to counter the extra weather helm. The increase or decrease in the wind and the resultant change in tiller line tension do not always match the increase or decrease in weather helm. When they do not the tension of the tiller line has to be balanced not merely by the pressure on the tiller resulting from weather helm but also by a rubber shock-cord. A system can then be built up whereby the sail steers the boat in winds of greatly varying strengths.*

A further refinement to the system shown here is to fit a counterweight to the storm jib so that heeling does not affect it. Otherwise the sail would hang down when the boat heeled and the rudder would be deflected undesirably. The sail can also be overbalanced so that the rudder is automatically deflected further as she heels, and thus counters the increase in weather helm. Fitting a second tiller line builds up a wind vane gear similar to 'Miranda'. This is suitable for an emergency but a proper wind vane gear is of course preferable for permanent use. It is rare to have a special sail for steering because one of the boat's normal sails can generally be used for this purpose.

sheet is made fast to the windward side of the tiller. The system works in winds of widely varying strengths without requiring adjustment, and course correction is both positive and very quick to take effect. Naturally a staysail can be used instead of the genoa and works in the same way. Other sails can be used similarly for all the points of sailing between a beam reach and a dead run, and the various methods possible are shown in figures 8.7 and 8.8.

It is more difficult to explain how a sail steers on a close hauled course. Most boats steer

Continued on page 116

tiller
line

8.3. *If a boat will not stay on course as a result of trimming the sails and giving the rudder appropriate bias her balance can be improved by setting a special sail. With the wind abeam, when the boat has great weather helm and maximum steering force is required, a good deal of this griping force can be countered by setting a jib boomed out to windward, either close forward of the mast as shown here or hanked to the forestay. In the latter case a very long boom is needed to hold the clew of the jib far enough forward and to windward if the system is to be used with the wind abeam. Figures 8.4C and 8.8A show a rig for a dead run using the jib in this figure, while figure 8.8D shows such a jib steering the boat.*

8.4. *The rigs shown here are all able to keep a boat on course. Some boats can steer themselves perfectly using these systems, or that in figure 8.3.* SPRAY, *in which Joshua Slocum sailed alone around the world, is a well-known example. She steered herself the whole way with her sails suitably trimmed and her rudder lashed. Slocum stepped a small mizzen on her afterdeck purely to improve her self-steering qualities.*

In cases when a wind vane gear just will not work altering the trim of the sails can help the boat to achieve a state where she can be steered by the vane.

Here the tiller is fixed, and it is simply due to the set of the sails that the boat stays on course. The aerodynamic forces on the rig have to balance the hydrodynamic forces on the underwater body.

One disadvantage of the systems drawn here is the relationship between course and wind strength. A new state of equilibrium has to be found every time the wind speed changes and, because the sails and the rudder are fixed, this can only be achieved by altering course. If the boat is to keep to her original course either the trim of the sails or the angle of the rudder has to be altered.

A To obtain directional stability on a close hauled course the genoa is hardened in too much and the mainsheet is slackened slightly. Most boats will stay on course when their

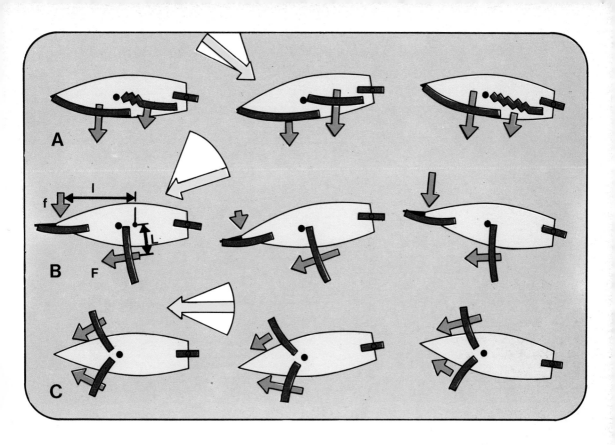

sails are trimmed like this and their rudders are fixed. When the boat bears away the mainsail fills and the lift force increases. Because the genoa had been hardened in too far the lift force produced was reduced in its partially stalled state and bearing away accentuates this. The air flow on the lee side of the sail becomes very turbulent, the sail stalls completely and the lift force is reduced even further. Pressure forward decreases, pressure aft increases and the boat is turned back to her original course. On the other hand when the boat luffs up the mainsail starts to shake and practically all lift force is lost, while the genoa sets perfectly at the optimum angle of incidence and the lift force increases. Pressure aft decreases, pressure forward increases, and the boat bears away back to her old course.

    In gusty weather light sensitive boats can luff too far in a gust and the genoa will start to shake. The boat will come

to a halt head to wind, or may even go about. Some other form of self-steering is required for this type of boat.

B   The system used by SPRAY and other boats is practicable on a reach. A small jib is sheeted hard amidships and the mainsail drives the boat forward. When the boat luffs the pressure on the jib increases and the mainsail becomes less efficient, but the opposite occurs when the boat bears away. This continues until a state of equilibrium, $F \times L = f \times l$, is reached and the aerodynamic forces balance the hydrodynamic forces.

C   Twin headsails set well forward in a vee will keep the boat on course on a dead run. The jib sheets may be attached to the tiller but this is not necessary if the vee is sufficiently acute.

    All the systems shown will be less dependent on the wind strength if one of the sails is connected to the helm with a tiller line.

8.5. *A two-masted boat has more sails to set, and this increases the alternatives when trimming her to sail a steady course and also when using special sails to steer her. A shows how the staysail and mizzen are trimmed for stability. They work in just the same way as the sloop's sails in figure 8.4A, the mizzen being eased out too far and the staysail hardened in too much. The genoa and mainsail are trimmed to provide propulsive force. The boat can sometimes sail a steady course when the wind is abeam, as seen at B. This was the principle used aboard* SPRAY. *The mizzen is set too far out and the staysail is trimmed practically amidships. Because the mizzen is right aft it is very sensitive to the alteration in the apparent wind which results from the stern yawing, as shown at A. As the boat bears away the stern swings to windward, causing the apparent wind to increase and blow from a more favourable angle. The lift force produced by the mizzen increases and tries to push the stern away. Setting the mizzen too far out increases this effect because the difference in lift force produced is then greater. Va = apparent wind on course. Va1 = wind resulting from the stern swinging. Va2 = new apparent wind. When the boat luffs the lift force produced by the mizzen is reduced.*

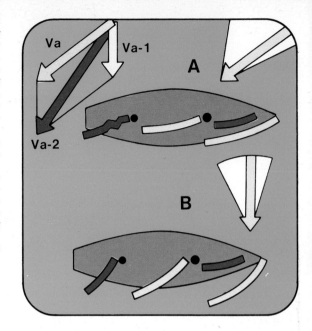

8.6. *Sails steering the boat when the wind is forward of the beam. The arrows indicate the wind direction that matches the way the sails are trimmed in the sketches, while the arcs show the range of wind direction through which the relevant systems can be used. To keep the sketches as simple as possible the sheet is shown leading direct to the tiller, although this is less likely in practice.*

A   *A staysail set aback is steering the boat, with the sheet attached to weather of the tiller. The staysail, operating like a large wind vane, corrects well and positively when the boat goes off course and when wind speed alters. Alterations in apparent wind speed resulting from altering course improve the effectiveness of this system. A jib set aback provides satisfactory steering power in light weather too, the only disadvantage being a reduction in speed because the jib is backed. This method can be used on virtually all points of sailing except dead before the wind, and because the jib operates the same way whatever the course no problem arises when a wind direction is reached when the sheet would have to be changed to the other side of the tiller as is the case with other systems.*

B   *The mainsail steers the boat. This is the best method with the wind forward of the beam. When the boat is pointing high the mainsail only reacts positively to an alteration in wind strength, corrections of deviation from course being left to* the boat's inherent stability. The mainsail will also bring the boat back on course when the wind becomes more free. The sheet can be made fast on the lee side of the tiller balanced by elastic when close hauled and the mainsail will then act like a large wind vane, operating as in figure 8.4A, but weather helm will not then be corrected automatically. The trim of the sails determines how well the mainsail will steer when the boat is on the wind, and this will decide whether the sheet is made fast to windward or to leeward of the tiller.

The mizzen or a genoa can also be used when the wind is forward of the beam but these methods are not included here because they are not always reliable.

C   *The tiller here extends aft of the stock to provide alternative points to which the sheet can be made fast. A rubber strop centralises the tiller continuously, which is more convenient when beating because the tension is adjusted to suit both port and starboard tacks and need not be touched.*

D   *Braine gear. Here the mainsheet is made fast to the tiller in such a way that, if the boat tacks accidentally, she will automatically be put about again on to the original tack. Alternatively the gear can be set so that the boat will sail on either tack, and she can therefore be put about without the need to adjust the lines on the new tack.*

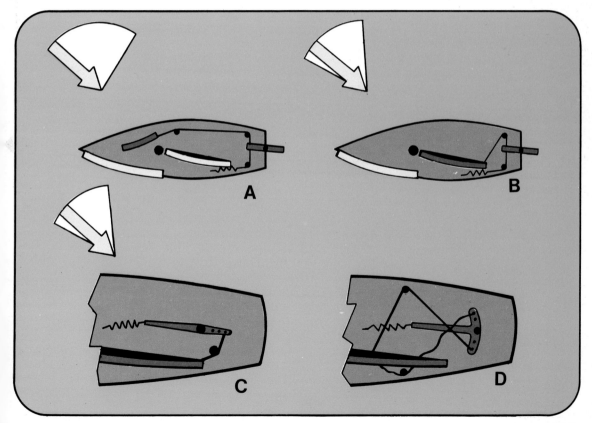

A

B

C

D

themselves anyway on this point of sailing, and the sail is used to transmit the change in wind strength to the rudder so that the necessary correction is made to counter the variation in weather helm. Figure 8.6 shows various possibilities that can be used when close hauled. A staysail set aback as in figure 8.3 will also correct effectively when wind strength changes and when the boat goes off course, acting in the same way as just described for the genoa when the wind is free. If the mainsail is used to steer only changes in wind strength are corrected, while the boat's inherent directional stability is relied on to correct a deviation from course. When the mainsheet is not hardened in fully on a close hauled course the mainsail will behave as described in figure 8.4A. Bearing away will increase the pull on the mainsheet and so the sheet has to be attached to the leeward side of the rudder. On the other hand if the sheet is attached to windward and the mainsail is hardened in slightly too much the effect is reversed, bearing away causes the angle of incidence to increase, the sail stalls completely and the lift force is reduced, whereas luffing up sets the sail at the optimum angle of incidence and the lift force increases. If the boat luffs too far the lift force will again decrease. In practice making the sheet fast to windward enables deviations from course to be corrected, even when pointing high on the wind. The aerodynamic forces on the rig resulting from going off course appear to override any possible wrong rudder reactions caused by the mainsheet.

The sheet is normally used as the tiller line, but naturally any line can be used provided that tension alters when the boat deviates from her course.

Various combinations of sails, tiller lines, rubber strops and tiller can be used, and a steering system using sails can always be assembled for a boat by going out sailing and observing how the tension of the sheets alters when she bears away and luffs up.

The system in use

An automatic pilot or a wind vane gear is naturally easier to use and requires less work, but this does not alter the fact that sailing boats making long passages should be able to use their sails for steering. Anyone who sails on a tight budget finds steering with sails a very attractive alternative to a wind vane gear.

At the start much patience and ingenuity is needed before a satisfactory method of using sails for steering is found, but the time spent is very worth while, particularly when sailing alone or with a small crew. It is much more pleasant to spend a few hours thinking out the self-steering system and getting the sails to do the work than to sit eternally locked to the helm. As already said, on the second occasion it takes little time to get the sails to steer the boat if you can remember the setting used before. Do not lose heart if the system did not work the first time because a solution can always be found.

Tiller lines and elastic

The tiller line, and sometimes the sheet itself are made fast to one side of the tiller. The pull exerted by this line is opposed by the boat's inherent weather helm. Sometimes weather helm is able to counteract the pull on the tiller line but, more often, the help of an elastic rubber strop is required to achieve a balance. If the pull on the tiller line is reduced when the boat goes off course the elastic pulls the tiller over, and vice versa, thus bringing her back on course.

It is largely the pull of the elastic that determines how well the system works, and the quality of this rubber shock cord is vital. If the rubber does not stretch easily the tiller line will not be able to pull hard enough to move the rudder, but if the rubber is too stretchy the tiller will move

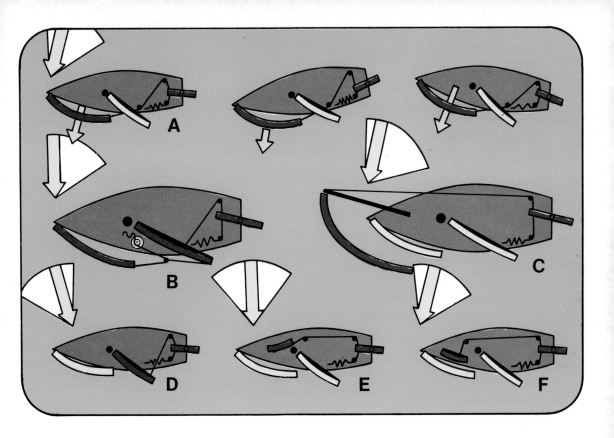

8.7. There are various ways of getting the boat to steer herself when the wind is abaft the beam. The most practicable methods are amongst those shown here and in every case the sheet is made fast to the windward side of the tiller.

A   The genoa steers the boat, and the way it works is described fully in the text. Luffing up increases the lift force produced while bearing away reduces the lift force. This system is used when the wind is abaft the beam.

B   Genoa and mainsail keep the boat on course. It is difficult to steer with sails when the wind is abeam, but by combining the pull of the mainsail and genoa sheets as shown here the sails can control the boat on a beam reach.

       It is hardly surprising that B is effective with a beam wind because it is a combination of a system that works well with the wind forward of the beam and a system that is effective when the wind is abaft the beam.

C   A reaching or running spinnaker steers the boat here. In light weather a reaching spinnaker can be effective, the guy being sheeted directly to the windward side of the tiller. The principle is the same as A, and this method is effective right round to a dead run.

D   The mainsail can keep the boat on course from high on the wind to a close reach. The way it operates has been described in figure 8.6.

E   A staysail set aback operates as described in figure 8.6A.

F   The staysail steers the boat in the same way as A. When the jib is set on a boom there are many ways of reducing the pull on the sheet to match it to the steering force required, and this explains why a boomed staysail is so often used to steer larger boats.

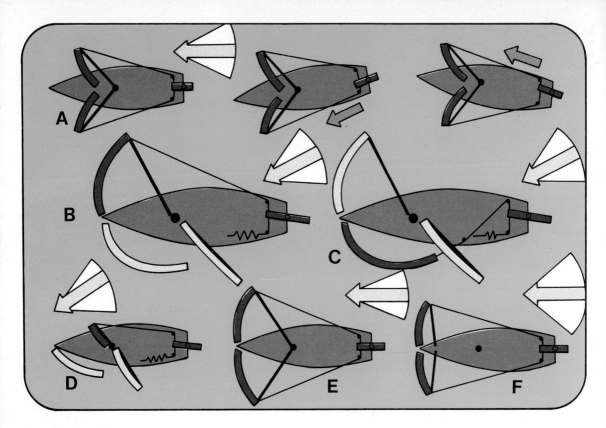

too far and oversteering will occur, the boat snaking either side of her course. The rubber must also stretch as evenly as possible. The shock cord, often used to lash sails and so on, is not very suitable when under load because it resists stretch initially and then extends more easily once a certain degree of load has been reached. It also has a limited life. Rubber strops such as those used for underwater weapons, catapults and so on stretch and retract much more evenly, and are thus better suited to the demands of self-steering gear.

Even more important than using good rubber is to keep friction as low as possible. The rudder itself and the sheaves over which the tiller lines run must move absolutely freely. Keep the number of blocks to a minimum when leading the lines to the tiller, and ensure that the sheaves are large enough and turn easily.

Tiller or wheel

When using a sail to steer it is preferable to have a tiller rather than a wheel, quite apart from the fact that it is easier to make steering lines fast to a tiller. If the boat has a wheel the tiller lines are often attached to the emergency tiller and, sometimes, the wheel can be uncoupled from the

8.8. Twin headsails can be used downwind to get the boat to steer herself and no elastic is required because both sheets are led to the tiller. If the wind is not absolutely dead aft the boat can be steered as described in figure 8.7.

A   Twin headsails set in a vee work as described in figure 8.4C. The luff runs from the top of the mast to a point close forward of the mast. The clews are held out by booms attached to the mast, a method which provides great stability and which is easy to handle. The only disadvantage is that the arc through which the booms can swing is restricted by the standing rigging and this is why this method is only suitable for running dead before the wind.

B   Genoa to windward. A second genoa boomed out to windward can steer the boat remarkably well on a broad reach. No extra equipment is needed and the mainsail need not be lowered. Twin headsails are preferable for longer periods, but the method shown here can be recommended for shorter spells and less work is required to set it up.

C   Genoa to leeward. If the wind is too far aft to set the sails as in figure 8.7A booming out a genoa to windward balances the rig again, while the genoa to leeward can steer the boat.

D   Jib to windward. A small jib hoisted up the leading side of the mast and boomed out to windward steers effectively and works in just the same way as the staysail set aback in figure 8.7E.

E   Twin headsails, hanked to the forestay, are held out here by booms attached to the mast. This is a simple method but very long booms are needed and, again, their freedom of movement is restricted by the mast's standing rigging.

F   Twin headsails are again hanked to the forestay but, because the booms are attached to the foredeck, the arc through which they can swing is increased and consequently this method can be used through a wider range of wind directions. The booms can be shorter than those attached to the mast and in strong winds the clews can be allowed to move forward to give the stability provided by A.

rudder stock so that the inertia resulting from turning the wheel at the same time as the rudder does not affect the system adversely. If this is impossible the tiller line can be made fast to a drum connected to the wheel.

Atoms and Aries wind vane gears, among others, manufacture a drum for use with their wind vanes, and these can obviously also be used when steering with sails.

Steering power

The steering power required is not very great, but the pull exerted by a sheet can be extremely high and far exceed the steering power needed. Only in smaller boats can the sheet be made fast directly to the tiller. The various fittings and rubber strops would be disproportionately heavy if they were to be adequate to deal with the very great pull exerted in larger boats. The sketches that set out the various methods all show the sheet leading directly to the tiller where it can be made fast with, say, a clove hitch. Figures 8.10 and 8.9C
Continued on page 122

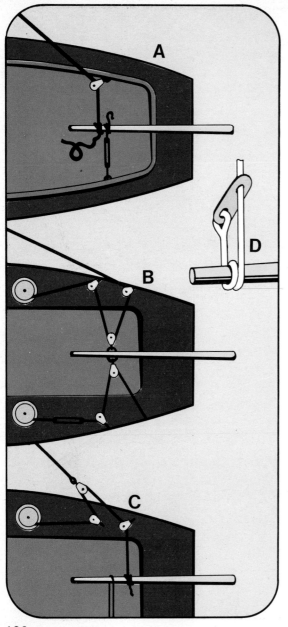

8.9. *Various methods of making the sheet (or tiller line) fast to the tiller.*

A The sheet leads direct to the helm where it is made fast with a clove hitch. This is only possible with small boats when there is little pull on the sheet. In larger boats the pull has to be reduced before making the sheet fast to the tiller.

B The sheet leads through a block on the tiller to a winch and this enables the tension of both the sheet and the elastic to be regulated exactly. This is a particularly popular method for twin headsails.

C The sheet is connected to the helm with a block and tackle which halves the pull on the sheet, making adjustment with the winch easy.

D A simple method of regulating the tension in either sheet or elastic.

8.10. *Various methods of making the tiller line fast to the sheet.*

A The tiller line can be made fast to the standing part of the mainsheet tackle. If the mainsheet is under great tension the tiller line pulls the standing part slightly out of line, and only a small part of the tension of the sheet is transmitted to the tiller line and therefore to the helm. When the wind is abeam or in light weather the sheet is uncleated and the tiller line takes over. Naturally the running part of the mainsheet tackle can also be used as a tiller line. If the mainsheet tackle has two running parts yet another method is possible, one part being made fast to the tiller while the other part regulates sheet tension. The sheeting tackle of jibs set on booms can also be used in this way.

B The running part of a tackle is used as the tiller line. The tackle is itself attached to the sheet. The pull on the sheet can be reduced as many times as the number of sheaves incorporated.

C If there is sufficient room between the genoa fairlead and the winch the tiller line can be attached directly to the sheet and will pull it out of line. When the pull on the sheet increases it will tend to straighten and vice versa, and this movement is transmitted to the helm by the tiller line.

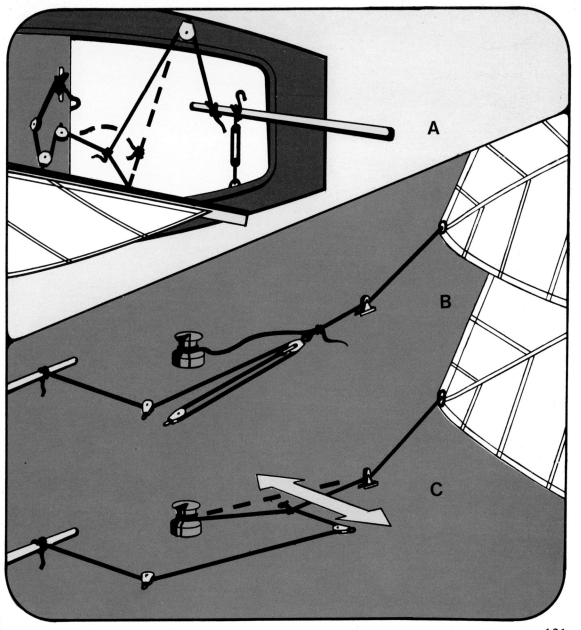

A

B

C

show how a tiller line can be attached to a sheet so that only a part of the sheet's pull is used to steer the boat. If a special tiller line like this is used the self-steering system can be disconnected immediately without touching the sails, and this is an important safety factor, for example if the boat finds herself on a collision course.

It is worth recommending that rudder movement should be limited when the sails are steering so as to reduce the possibility of oversteering. A maximum deflection of 5°–10° to port and starboard should be satisfactory on a reach. Rudder deflection can be restricted by attaching two lines to the tiller to limit its travel, or by using pegs either side. Two pieces of strong rubber are better than two lines because shocks transmitted to the rudder are avoided. This is valid when fixing the rudder too. If the rudder and the fittings that hold it fast are very heavy it is preferable to use very strong elastic either side of the tiller to restrain it.

Adjustment

Sheet (tiller line) tension depends on the wind strength. It is not only when the boat goes off course that sheet tension alters but also when the wind increases in strength, and self-steering gear therefore has to be adjusted to every change of wind. This is partly countered by a boat's inherent weather helm. When the wind blows more strongly, the pull on the tiller line becomes greater but weather helm also always increases and the helm has to be deflected further if the boat is to stay on course. It is possible to find a setting that provides directional stability over a great range of wind speeds by experimenting with the point where the steering line is made fast to the tiller, with the elasticity of the rubber strops, and with the degree of tension on both tiller line and rubber strop. If the boat keeps luffing up when the wind blows harder the tension of tiller line and rubber

strop should both be increased, but if she tends to bear away slacken them slightly. Unless a balance between weather helm, wind strength and the pull of the sheet is found continual alterations have to be made to the rubber strop tension.

In light weather the rubber strop should be eased off with the tiller slightly to leeward so that an increase in wind speed will automatically result in the tiller being pulled to windward by the extra tension on the sheet. This is required to counter the increase in weather helm, the pull of the tiller line being balanced by pressure on the rudder and the pull of the rubber strop which is now stretched.

Altering the position where the rubber strop is attached to the tiller among other things affects the reaction of the elastic. Heavy rubber made fast close to the rudder stock will have the same effect as rubber that gives more easily made fast to the forward end of the tiller. The latter is better from the point of view of adjustment, and there is less load on the point where it is attached. This is equally true of the tiller line, and a light pull that moves the line a greater distance is preferable. What is possible depends on the way in which the changes in tiller line tension are transmitted to the sheet.

In some cases no rubber strop is needed, the pull of the tiller line being countered only by pressure on the rudder, but this is really only possible when increases and decreases in wind strength, and the consequent changes in tiller line tension, are balanced by the change in weather helm, and thus the pressure on the rudder. In most boats the pressure on the helm has to be augmented by a rubber strop if a system is to be set up that does not require resetting every time the wind strength alters.

Choice

The systems that use the mainsail give the best

results close hauled (figure 8.6) and the mainsail can be used to steer the boat until the apparent wind's direction is just forward of the beam. When the wind is abaft the beam a genoa or staysail do the job well (figure 8.7A). The genoa can still be used on a run provided that the rig is balanced by setting a jib to windward (figure 8.8C). A small sail set to windward, as in figure 8.8D and 8.3, also gives good results. For long stretches dead before the wind the mainsail can be lowered and replaced by twin headsails (figures 8.8A, E and F).

For general use a staysail set aback as in figure 8.6A and figure 8.7E can steer the boat on practically all points of sailing.

Advantages and disadvantages

Using sails to steer the boat poses problems for single-handed sailors when changing sails or reefing because, obviously, they cannot operate at that moment whereas wind vanes and automatic pilots continue to keep the boat on course. Gusty winds also cause a lot of work because the sails have to be adjusted both to the wind direction and, to a lesser degree, to wind strength. Changing course therefore takes a long time whereas with automatic pilots and wind vanes, all that is often needed is to turn a knob or to pull a line from the protection of the cabin. When sails are steering it takes time to find the correct tension for the rubber strop and tiller line before the boat settles on her new course.

Steering with sails, or knowing how to adapt the rig to steer the boat, is important when making long ocean passages, whatever the boat, and can be used as a reserve self-steering system should other methods fail. The loss of speed that may result when sails are steering—and this is by no means always the case—is a small price to pay for the extra comfort, particularly when this comfort costs so little money.

Appendix 1

Classification of wind vane steering gears

Sensor
1. vertical axis vane
2. inclined axis vane
3. horizontal axis vane
4. dual vertical axis vane
5. windmill vane
6. counterweight on vane, trim tab or pendulum
7. wind-driven gyroscope
8. towed line

Multiplication of force
1. trim tab
2. pendulum with horizontal axis
   a. unbalanced
   b. partially balanced
3. pendulum with vertical axis

Steering
1. main rudder
2. auxiliary rudder
   a. unbalanced
   b. partially balanced
   c. completely balanced
   d. overbalanced
   e. with skeg
   f. as a single unit with the keel

Course adjustment
1. graduated
2. continuous
   a. remote control
   b. no remote control

Characteristics
1. countering of yawing

    a. strong
    b. positive
    c. neutral
    d. none
2. steering force
    a. large
    b. small
3. rudder deflection
    a. in proportion to course error
    b. not in proportion
4. speed of reaction
    a. high
    b. normal
    c. low

Appendix 2

Bibliography

Self-Steering The Amateur Yacht Research Society, Woodacres, Hythe, Kent, England, 2nd edition 1970.

A collection of ideas, letters and diagrams of wind vanes and self-steering by means of sails. The great amount of practical information and original ideas makes up for the lack of background theory. The problems are considered entirely on the basis of experience.

Self-steering for sailing craft Dr. John S. Letcher Jr. International Marine Publishing Co, Camden, Maine, USA. 1st edition 1974.

The first book to give the theoretical background to the behaviour of wind vane gears and steering with the help of sails. Dr. Letcher explains the how and why of self-steering in a way that is easily understood by anyone who is at all interested. The 25,000 miles that the author has sailed guarantees the practical application of the theory in this book. The information is essential for every private or professional person wishing to design a self-steering gear.

Pen Duick Eric Tabarly, Adlard Coles Ltd. London, England. 1st edition 1970, Chapter 7. (Out of print.)

Chapter 7 covers the self-steering gears fitted to the many *Pen Duick*s. The description of the MNOP wind vanes is clear but brief.

Skene's element of yacht design F. S. Kinney, Dodd, Mead & Co. New York, USA, 8th edition, 1973. Chapter 16.

A close look at the use of a trim tab to operate the rudder, whether powered by a wind vane, an automatic pilot or manually.

The behaviour and stability of wind operated steering systems for yachts A. L. Buchan, J. R. Flewitt, Southampton University Yacht Research report no. 27, 1st edition 1968.

A mathematical approach to the behaviour of wind vane gears.

Theory of wing sections I. H. Abbott, A. E. von Doenhoff, Dover Publications Inc, New York, 1st edition 1958.

As well as a broad view of theory this book gives the most frequently used NACA profile shapes that are suitable for vanes and rudders.

Windvaanstuurinrichtingen G. Dijkstra, Maandblad Watersport 1973/4.

A series of four articles which briefly cover the contents of this book.

Appendix 3

List of illustrations

127